Diabetic Dessert Cookbook

Discover the Joy of Baking with Recipes Designed for Health, Flavor, and Easy Preparation for Every Diabetic's Dietary Needs

Averill Vang

Table of Contents

INTRODUCTION 13

THE IMPORTANCE OF MANAGING DIABETES THROUGH DIET...13

UNDERSTANDING DIABETES: TYPES 1, 2, AND GESTATIONAL 15

HOW TO USE THIS COOKBOOK...17

CHAPTER 1: UNDERSTANDING SUGAR SUBSTITUTES AND THEIR CONTRAINDICATIONS 19

TYPES OF SUGAR SUBSTITUTES: NATURAL VS. ARTIFICIAL 19

HOW TO CHOOSE THE RIGHT SUGAR SUBSTITUTE FOR YOUR DESSERT............................20

CONTRAINDICATIONS AND WHAT TO WATCH OUT FOR..22

CHAPTER 2: FLOUR POWER: CHOOSING THE RIGHT FLOUR FOR DIABETIC DESSERTS 25

WHOLE GRAINS VS. REFINED FLOURS: WHAT'S BEST FOR BLOOD SUGAR CONTROL..............25

ALMOND, COCONUT, AND OTHER LOW-CARB FLOUR ALTERNATIVES....................................27

GLUTEN-FREE BAKING FOR DIABETICS 28

CHAPTER 3: CAKES & CUPCAKES FOR EVERY OCCASION 31

LOW-CARB SPONGE CAKE BASICS 31

Recipe 1: Vanilla Almond Sponge Cake 31

Recipe 2: Lemon Zest Sponge Cake 31

Recipe 3: Chocolate Hazelnut Sponge Cake 31

Recipe 4: Cinnamon Apple Sponge Cake 31

Recipe 5: Coconut Lime Sponge Cake 32

Recipe 6: Pumpkin Spice Sponge Cake 32

DECORATING DIABETIC-FRIENDLY CAKES 33

Recipe 1: Vanilla Bean Cream Cheese Frosting 33

Recipe 2: Chocolate Avocado Ganache...33

Recipe 3: Berry Compote Topping...33

Recipe 4: Almond Crunch Topping 34

Recipe 5: Coconut Cream Frosting 34

Recipe 6: Lemon Zest Glaze..34

Recipe 7: Sugar-Free Sprinkles 34

SPECIAL OCCASION SHOWSTOPPERS 35

Recipe 1: Triple Berry Layer Cake 35

Recipe 2: Chocolate-Hazelnut Torte 35

Recipe 3: Lemon Almond Pavlova 36

Recipe 4: Decadent Flourless Chocolate Cake 36

Recipe 5: Vanilla Bean Cheesecake with Almond Crust 36

Recipe 6: Red Velvet Cupcakes with Cream Cheese Frosting 36

Recipe 7: Pear and Ginger Spice Cake 37

CHAPTER 4: COOKIES & BARS FOR EASY SNACKING **39**

CRUNCHY AND CRISPY 39

Recipe 1: Almond Flour Sesame Crackers 39

Recipe 2: Crunchy Peanut Butter Cookies 39

Recipe 3: Cheddar Almond Flour Crackers 40

Recipe 4: Cinnamon Pecan Brittle 40

Recipe 5: Coconut Crisps 40

Recipe 6: Parmesan Rosemary Crisps 41

Recipe 7: Spicy Pumpkin Seeds 41

SOFT AND CHEWY BARS FOR ENERGY BOOSTS 42

Recipe 1: No-Bake Peanut Butter Chocolate Chip Bars 42

Recipe 2: Chewy Almond Joy Bars 42

Recipe 3: Pumpkin Spice Protein Bars 42

Recipe 4: Lemon Cashew Energy Bars 43

Recipe 5: Cinnamon Roll Protein Bars 43

Recipe 6: Berry Bliss Granola Bars 43

Recipe 7: Dark Chocolate Mint Protein Bars 44

NO-BAKE COOKIES AND BARS 44

Recipe 1: Cocoa Almond Protein Balls 44

Recipe 2: Lemon Cashew Coconut Bars 45

Recipe 3: Peanut Butter Hemp Seed Cookies 45

Recipe 4: Berry Bliss Bars 45

Recipe 5: No-Bake Chocolate Walnut Brownies 46

Recipe 6: Matcha Green Tea Energy Squares 46

Recipe 7: Spiced Pumpkin Seed and Nut Bars 46

CHAPTER 5: PIES & TARTS THAT PLEASE EVERY PALATE **49**

SAVORY PIES FOR ANY MEAL 49

Recipe 1: Mediterranean Vegetable Quiche 49

Recipe 2: Spinach and Mushroom Breakfast Pie 49

Recipe 3: Low-Carb Chicken Pot Pie 50

Recipe 4: Cheesy Broccoli Bacon Quiche 50

Recipe 5: Savory Turkey and Veggie Tart 50

Recipe 6: Beef and Mushroom Shepherd's Pie 51

Recipe 7: Zucchini and Tomato Tart with Mozzarella 51

SWEET AND FRUITY TART MAKEOVERS 52

Recipe 1: Berry Bliss Tart 52

Recipe 2: Lemon Almond Tart 52

Recipe 3: Rustic Apple Cinnamon Tart 52

Recipe 4: No-Bake Coconut Mango Tart 53

Recipe 5: Chocolate Raspberry Dream Tart 53

Recipe 6: Key Lime Avocado Tart 53

Recipe 7: Strawberry Basil Balsamic Tart 54

CLASSIC PIES WITH A DIABETIC-FRIENDLY TWIST 54

Recipe 1: Keto Apple Pie 54

Recipe 2: Sugar-Free Pumpkin Pie 55

Recipe 3: Low-Carb Pecan Pie 55

Recipe 4: Lemon Meringue Pie (Low-Carb) 55

Recipe 5: Raspberry Almond Tart 56

Recipe 6: Chocolate Silk Pie 56

Recipe 7: Key Lime Pie 56

CHAPTER 6: MUFFINS & BREADS FOR BREAKFAST OR TEA TIME 57

HIGH-FIBER MUFFINS FOR A HEALTHY START 57

Recipe 1: Chia & Blueberry Muffins 57

Recipe 2: Flaxseed & Walnut Breakfast Muffins 57

Recipe 3: Apple Cinnamon Fiber Muffins 58

Recipe 4: Pumpkin Seed & Avocado Oil Muffins 58

Recipe 5: Carrot & Ginger Fiber Muffins 59

Recipe 6: Spicy Zucchini Oat Muffins 59

Recipe 7: Cocoa & Beet Fiber Muffins 60

SWEET AND SAVORY QUICK BREADS 60

Recipe 1: Zucchini Cheddar Bread 60

Recipe 2: Lemon Poppy Seed Loaf 61

Recipe 3: Cranberry Walnut Bread 61

Recipe 4: Savory Olive and Herb Bread 62

Recipe 5: Cinnamon Swirl Breakfast Bread 62

Recipe 6: Blueberry Lemon Loaf 63

Recipe 7: Choco-Almond Banana Bread 63

TEA TIME TREATS: SCONES AND BISCOTTI 64

Recipe 1: Almond Flour Lemon Scones 64

Recipe 2: Cranberry Orange Biscotti 64

Recipe 3: Coconut Chia Seed Scones 65

Recipe 4: Espresso Chocolate Biscotti 65

Recipe 5: Lemon Lavender Scones 65

Recipe 6: Pistachio Rosewater Biscotti 66

Recipe 7: Cheddar and Chive Scones 66

CHAPTER 7: FROZEN TREATS TO BEAT THE HEAT **67**

SUGAR-FREE ICE CREAMS AND SORBETS 67

Recipe 1: Creamy Avocado Lime Ice Cream 67

Recipe 2: Berry Blast Sorbet 67

Recipe 3: Chocolate Peanut Butter Keto Ice Cream 67

Recipe 4: Mint Chocolate Chip Ice Cream 68

Recipe 5: Cinnamon Toast Ice Cream 68

Recipe 6: Tropical Mango Sorbet 68

Recipe 7: Raspberry Lemonade Ice Cream 68

FROZEN YOGURT AND POPSICLES 69

Recipe 1: Greek Yogurt Berry Popsicles 69

Recipe 2: Keto Chocolate Fudge Pops 69

Recipe 3: Lemon Cucumber Mint Yogurt Pops 70

Recipe 4: Avocado Lime Frozen Yogurt 70

Recipe 5: Strawberry Basil Popsicles 70

Recipe 6: Coconut Almond Swirl Frozen Yogurt 70

Recipe 7: Peach Ginger Yogurt Pops 71

DIABETIC-FRIENDLY ICE CREAM CAKE 71

Recipe 1: Vanilla Berry Layer Ice Cream Cake 71

Recipe 2: Keto Chocolate Peanut Butter Ice Cream Cake 72

Recipe 3: Mint Chocolate Chip Ice Cream Cake 72

Recipe 4: Strawberry Cheesecake Ice Cream Cake 73

Recipe 5: Lemon Blueberry Ice Cream Cake 73

Recipe 6: Coffee Almond Fudge Ice Cream Cake 74

Recipe 7: Raspberry Ripple Ice Cream Cake 74

CHAPTER 8: FESTIVE DESSERTS FOR SPECIAL OCCASIONS **77**

ELEGANT DESSERTS FOR FORMAL GATHERINGS 77

Recipe 1: Raspberry Almond Frangipane Tart 77

Recipe 2: Chocolate Avocado Mousse with Hazelnut Crunch 77

Recipe 3: Lemon Lavender Panna Cotta 78

Recipe 4: Keto Opera Cake 78

Recipe 5: Saffron and Cardamom Infused Berry Compote over Greek Yogurt 78

Recipe 6: Keto Tiramisu 79

Recipe 7: Pistachio Rosewater Pavlova 79

HOLIDAY TREATS EVERYONE CAN ENJOY 79

Recipe 1: Gingerbread Keto Cookies 79

Recipe 2: Pumpkin Spice Cheesecake Bites 80

Recipe 3: Sugar-Free Peppermint Mocha Truffles 80

Recipe 4: Holiday Spiced Nut Mix 80

Recipe 5: Eggnog Panna Cotta 81

Recipe 6: Cranberry Orange Relish 81

Recipe 7: Low-Carb Yule Log 81

CELEBRATORY CAKES WITHOUT THE SUGAR CRASH 82

Recipe 1: Almond Joy Layer Cake 82

Recipe 2: Lemon Raspberry Cheesecake 82

Recipe 3: Classic Keto Vanilla Cake 83

Recipe 4: Chocolate Hazelnut Torte 83

Recipe 5: Strawberries and Cream Sponge Cake 83

Recipe 6: Spiced Carrot Cake with Cream Cheese Frosting 84

Recipe 7: Keto Black Forest Cake 84

CHAPTER 9: INTERNATIONAL DESSERTS WITH A DIABETIC TWIST **85**

EUROPEAN DELIGHTS WITH A HEALTHY TWIST 85

Recipe 1: Keto Tiramisu 85

Recipe 2: French Lemon Tart with Almond Crust 85

Recipe 3: Spanish Almond Cake 85

Recipe 4: Keto Black Forest Cake 86

Recipe 5: Italian Ricotta Cheesecake 86

Recipe 6: Austrian Linzer Torte 86

Recipe 7: Greek Yogurt Panna Cotta 86

ASIAN-INSPIRED SUGAR-FREE SWEETS 87

Recipe 1: Keto Matcha Green Tea Cheesecake 87

Recipe 2: Sugar-Free Coconut Milk Mango Mochi 87

Recipe 3: Keto Sesame Seed Balls (Jian Dui) 87

Recipe 4: Diabetic-Friendly Sweet Potato Mooncakes 87

Recipe 5: Sugar-Free Lychee Jelly 88

Recipe 6: Keto Almond Jelly (Annin Tofu) 88

Recipe 7: Sugar-Free Matcha Ice Cream 88

MIDDLE EASTERN DESSERTS FOR DIABETIC DIETS 89

Recipe 1: Keto Baklava Bites 89

Recipe 2: Sugar-Free Pistachio Halva 89

Recipe 3: Low-Carb Rosewater and Saffron Mousse 89

Recipe 4: Keto Date and Walnut Bars 90

Recipe 5: Almond and Orange Flourless Cake 90

Recipe 6: Sugar-Free Lebanese Nights (Layali Lubnan) 90

Recipe 7: Creamy Cardamom Rose Flavored Yogurt 91

CHAPTER 10: SWEETS FOR GESTATIONAL DIABETES 93

NUTRIENT-RICH SNACKS FOR EXPECTING MOTHERS 93

Recipe 1: Avocado and Egg Salad Cups 93

Recipe 2: Spinach and Feta Stuffed Mushrooms 93

Recipe 3: Greek Yogurt and Berry Parfait 93

Recipe 4: Quinoa and Black Bean Salad 94

Recipe 5: Almond Butter and Banana Smoothie 94

Recipe 6: Cottage Cheese and Peach Compote 94

Recipe 7: Chia Seed and Coconut Milk Pudding 95

QUICK AND EASY MEALS FOR BUSY MOMS-TO-BE 95

Recipe 1: Turkey and Quinoa Stuffed Peppers 95

Recipe 2: Spinach and Mushroom Frittata 95

Recipe 3: Avocado Chicken Salad 96

Recipe 4: Salmon and Asparagus One-Pan Dinner 96

Recipe 5: Zucchini Noodles with Pesto Chicken 96

Recipe 6: Quick Veggie Stir-Fry with Tofu 97

Recipe 7: Beef and Broccoli Bowl 97

SWEET INDULGENCES THAT FIT YOUR DIET 98

Recipe 1: Almond Flour Chocolate Chip Cookies 98

Recipe 2: Berry Chia Pudding 98

Recipe 3: Greek Yogurt Cheesecake with Strawberry Compote 98

Recipe 4: Lemon Ricotta Pancakes 99

Recipe 5: No-Bake Peanut Butter Energy Balls 99

Recipe 6: Avocado Chocolate Mousse 100

Recipe 7: Cinnamon Almond Flour Apple Crisp 100

CHAPTER 11: BUILDING A DIABETIC-FRIENDLY PANTRY **101**

ESSENTIAL INGREDIENTS FOR DIABETIC BAKING 101

READING LABELS: WHAT TO LOOK FOR AND WHAT TO AVOID 102

PLANNING AND PREPARING DIABETIC-FRIENDLY DESSERTS AHEAD OF TIME 103

CONCLUSION **105**

TIPS FOR ENJOYING DESSERTS WHILE MANAGING DIABETES 105

HOW TO ADAPT YOUR FAVORITE RECIPES TO BE MORE DIABETIC-FRIENDLY 106

ENCOURAGEMENT FOR A BALANCED AND SWEET LIFE 107

BONUS: SWEET SEASONS DIABETIC - FRIENDLY DESSERTS THROUGH THE YEAR............... 108

Introduction

The Importance of Managing Diabetes Through Diet

In the heart of a journey toward wellness, managing diabetes through the art and science of diet stands as a beacon of hope and transformation. This isn't merely about swapping sugar for sweeteners or counting carbohydrates with the precision of an accountant; it's an exploration into the very essence of nourishment, where every bite holds the potential to either fuel the delicate balance of blood sugar or tip the scales toward disparity.

At its core, diabetes management is an intimate dance with the food we eat, a dance that demands both knowledge and intuition. The food on our plates does more than satisfy hunger— it communicates with our bodies, sending signals that can either support our health or undermine it. For individuals navigating the complexities of diabetes, this conversation between food and physiology isn't just casual chatter; it's a critical dialogue that can dictate the quality of daily life and long-term wellbeing.

Why, you might ask, does diet wield such power in the realm of diabetes management? The answer lies in the body's ability to metabolize glucose—a simple sugar that serves as a primary energy source. For those living with diabetes, the body's relationship with glucose is strained, marked by an inability to regulate blood sugar levels effectively. Whether due to insufficient insulin production in Type 1 diabetes, the body's resistance to insulin in Type 2, or the temporary insulin resistance seen in gestational diabetes, the result is the same: glucose levels that stray from the norm, carrying the risk of health complications.

In the face of this challenge, diet emerges not just as a tool, but as a powerful ally. Through dietary choices, individuals have the opportunity to influence their blood sugar levels, steering them toward stability rather than fluctuation. But this isn't a journey of deprivation or rigid dietary confines; rather, it's an invitation to discover the richness of flavors and foods that nourish the body while respecting its unique needs.

Imagine, if you will, the vibrant colors of a farmer's market—the deep purples of berries, the bright greens of leafy vegetables, and the warm oranges of sweet potatoes. Each of these foods brings not just color to our plates, but a wealth of nutrients that support blood sugar management. Berries, with their antioxidants and fiber, offer sweetness without a rapid spike in glucose. Leafy greens, packed with vitamins and minerals, provide nourishment without excess calories or carbohydrates. Sweet potatoes, rich in fiber and complex carbohydrates, offer energy that releases slowly, preventing the sharp rises in blood sugar that can occur with more refined carbs.

Yet, managing diabetes through diet extends beyond the mere selection of foods; it's about understanding the rhythm and patterns of eating. The timing of meals, the balance of macronutrients, and the portion sizes all play pivotal roles in how food affects blood sugar. A breakfast rich in protein and healthy fats, for example, can provide a stable energy source that prevents the mid-morning blood sugar crash often seen with high-carbohydrate meals. A lunch balanced with complex carbohydrates, lean protein, and healthy fats can sustain energy levels and prevent the afternoon slump. Dinner, ideally lighter and earlier, can support blood sugar stability through the night, preventing the dawn phenomenon—a rise in glucose levels that occurs for some people with diabetes in the early morning hours.

But what of desserts, you might wonder? This is where the magic of culinary creativity shines brightest. Managing diabetes doesn't mean forsaking the joy of a sweet finish to a meal. Through the innovative use of natural sweeteners, fiber-rich flours, and healthy fats, desserts can be reimagined as not just permissible, but beneficial components of a diabetes-friendly diet. A dessert crafted with almond flour, sweetened with erythritol, and enriched with dark chocolate not only delights the palate but also aligns with the goals of blood sugar management.

This approach to managing diabetes through diet isn't about strict adherence to a list of "do's and don'ts." It's a philosophy of eating that celebrates diversity, listens to the body's cues, and finds joy in the nourishment of food. It acknowledges that each individual's journey with diabetes is unique, requiring personalized adjustments and an openness to experimentation.

In embracing this philosophy, we not only navigate the challenges of diabetes with grace but also discover a deeper appreciation for the food we eat. We learn that managing diabetes through diet is not a restrictive sentence, but a liberating journey toward wellness. It's a journey that doesn't just manage diabetes—it enriches life, one delicious, thoughtfully chosen bite at a time.

Thus, as we embark on this culinary adventure, let us remember that food is not just fuel; it is medicine, it is joy, and it is a vital part of the tapestry of our lives. With every meal, we have the opportunity to support our health, to delight our senses, and to honor the body's needs. In the management of diabetes, the role of diet is not just important—it is transformative, offering a pathway to health that is as flavorful as it is nourishing.

Understanding Diabetes: Types 1, 2, and Gestational

Embarking on a journey to demystify diabetes, it's imperative to weave through the tapestry of its types—Type 1, Type 2, and Gestational—each distinct in its origin, yet unified in the challenge it poses. This exploration isn't merely academic; it's a foundational step towards understanding how our choices, particularly dietary ones, can influence the trajectory of diabetes management. Through this lens, let's embark on a narrative that elucidates the essence of diabetes in its various forms, offering not just clarity but a beacon of hope for those navigating this path.

Type 1 diabetes emerges as an enigmatic challenge, where the body, in a twist of fate, turns against its insulin-producing cells in the pancreas. This autoimmune response leaves individuals with a life-long reliance on insulin therapy, as their bodies can no longer produce the hormone that acts as a key, unlocking cells to absorb glucose from the bloodstream. The management of Type 1 diabetes is a delicate ballet of balancing insulin with food intake and energy expenditure, a testament to human resilience and the power of precision in dietary choices.

Contrastingly, Type 2 diabetes paints a different picture, one where the body still produces insulin but has become desensitized to its effects—a state known as insulin resistance. This condition, often linked to lifestyle factors such as diet, physical inactivity, and obesity, highlights the profound impact of our daily choices on our health. The narrative of Type 2 diabetes is one of potential reversal or significant management through dietary modifications, physical activity, and, in some cases, medication. It's a story of empowerment, illustrating that through informed choices, individuals can influence the course of their condition.

Gestational diabetes, a temporary condition that emerges during pregnancy, introduces a unique set of considerations. It underscores the body's increased insulin demands during this critical time and the potential implications for both mother and child if these demands are not met. Gestational diabetes serves as a poignant reminder of the interconnectedness of our health and the ripple effects our physiological states can have on those we hold dear.

Understanding these types of diabetes is not just about recognizing their differences; it's about seeing the common thread they share in the significant role diet plays in their management. This knowledge brings into focus the importance of not just what we eat, but how we eat. It invites us to consider the timing of our meals, the balance of macronutrients, and the impact of food on our blood sugar levels. It's a call to action, urging us to forge a relationship with food that is both nurturing and mindful, recognizing its power to shape our health and wellbeing.

As we delve deeper into the nuances of managing diabetes, we encounter the concept of the glycemic index—a tool that measures how certain foods impact blood sugar levels. This tool becomes a compass, guiding us towards choices that support blood sugar stability. It's not about imposing restrictions but about expanding our culinary horizons to include foods that nourish and sustain us, foods that are allies in our journey towards health.

But the journey doesn't stop at understanding; it beckons us to action. It invites us into the kitchen, a place of transformation where ingredients come together not just to create meals, but to craft a lifestyle that embraces the full spectrum of flavors while honoring our bodies' needs. This is where the alchemy of cooking meets the science of nutrition, where the act of preparing a meal becomes an expression of self-care and a step towards wellness.

In this exploration of diabetes and its dietary management, we're reminded of the power of knowledge, the value of informed choices, and the impact of diet on our health. It's a narrative that transcends the individual, touching the lives of families and communities, weaving a collective story of resilience, empowerment, and hope.

Through this understanding, we pave the way for a deeper connection with our food and ourselves, fostering a relationship that is rooted in awareness and respect. It's a journey that doesn't just aim to manage diabetes but seeks to enhance the quality of life, proving that with the right knowledge and choices, we can navigate the complexities of diabetes with grace and strength.

As we stand at the crossroads of choice and consequence, let's choose the path that leads to wellness, armed with the knowledge that our decisions, particularly those related to diet, hold the key to not just managing diabetes, but thriving in spite of it. This is the heart of our exploration, a testament to the indomitable spirit of those who face diabetes not as a sentence, but as a challenge to be met with courage, knowledge, and hope.

How to Use This Cookbook

Diving into the heart of this cookbook, we find ourselves not just flipping through pages of recipes, but embarking on a transformative journey that marries the science of nutrition with the art of culinary creativity. This isn't just any cookbook; it's a guide, a companion, and a tool designed to navigate the nuanced and often misunderstood landscape of diabetes management through diet. Understanding how to wield this tool effectively is paramount in making the leap from mere survival to thriving with diabetes, regardless of its type.

At first glance, the cookbook presents itself as a collection of recipes. But to view it through such a narrow lens would be to miss the forest for the trees. This cookbook is a tapestry, each recipe a thread woven with care and intent, designed to enrich your dietary management of diabetes. The key to unlocking its full potential lies in understanding its structure and how it can be adapted to fit your unique dietary needs and preferences.

To begin, consider this cookbook as your culinary GPS, guiding you through the landscape of diabetic-friendly cuisine. Each recipe has been crafted not only with flavor in mind but with an eye towards nutritional balance, aiming to support stable blood glucose levels while delighting the palate. The recipes span a broad spectrum, from the simplicity of a morning smoothie to the complexity of a festive holiday dessert, ensuring that every meal can be a celebration of taste and health.

Navigating this cookbook effectively requires a blend of curiosity and mindfulness. Start by acquainting yourself with the introductory sections that lay the groundwork for diabetic dietary management. Here, you'll find insights into how various ingredients impact blood sugar levels and tips for meal planning and portion control—essential skills for anyone looking to manage diabetes through diet.

As you delve deeper, you'll notice that each recipe is accompanied by detailed nutritional information. This isn't merely for reference; it's a tool to help you understand the impact of each meal on your blood sugar management. By becoming familiar with these details, you can start to tailor your meals to fit your specific dietary needs, adjusting ingredients and portions as necessary to maintain your target blood glucose levels.

But this cookbook is more than just a collection of recipes and nutritional facts; it's an invitation to experiment and explore. The kitchen becomes your laboratory, each recipe an experiment in taste and nutrition. Don't be afraid to modify recipes based on your preferences or dietary requirements. Whether it's substituting a sweetener, swapping out a flour type, or adjusting portion sizes, each modification is a step towards personalizing your dietary management.

Engagement with this cookbook is also about embracing the broader context of your meals. It encourages you to consider not just what you're eating but how you're eating. The timing of meals, the combination of foods, and even the pace at which you eat can all influence your blood sugar levels. This holistic approach to meal planning and preparation is essential for anyone looking to manage their diabetes effectively.

Moreover, this cookbook is designed to grow with you. As you experiment with recipes and adapt them to your needs, you'll gain insights into your dietary preferences and how different foods impact your diabetes management. This process of exploration and adaptation is central to the cookbook's philosophy—it's not just about following recipes but about learning, adapting, and thriving.

Finally, this cookbook aims to build a community of support and inspiration. It's a shared space where individuals navigating the challenges of diabetes can find not just culinary inspiration but also a sense of belonging. Through the pages of this cookbook, you're invited to join a community that understands the intricacies of diabetes management and celebrates the joy of culinary exploration.

In essence, this cookbook is your companion on a journey towards a richer, more flavorful life with diabetes. It's a testament to the belief that managing diabetes through diet doesn't have to be about restriction and sacrifice but can be a journey of discovery, enjoyment, and empowerment. As you turn each page and try each recipe, remember that this cookbook is more than just a guide to diabetic-friendly cooking—it's a roadmap to a healthier, more vibrant life, one delicious meal at a time.

Chapter 1: Understanding Sugar Substitutes and Their Contraindications

Types of Sugar Substitutes: Natural vs. Artificial

In the vast world of culinary arts, the quest for the perfect sweetener is akin to a modern-day alchemy. This search is especially poignant for those navigating the complexities of diabetes management, where the choice of sweetener can significantly impact one's health and enjoyment of food. The dichotomy between natural and artificial sweeteners offers a landscape ripe for exploration, each with its own set of characteristics, benefits, and considerations.

Natural sweeteners, gifts from nature, are derived without synthetic processes, offering a semblance of purity in their essence. They include a diverse array of options, from the raw sweetness of honey and maple syrup to the subtle nuances of agave nectar and fruit juices. These sweeteners carry more than just sweetness; they bring with them a spectrum of flavors and nutritional profiles that can enhance a dessert not only with sugar but with depth and complexity.

However, their natural origin does not inherently crown them as the superior choice for all, especially for individuals with diabetes. Their impact on blood sugar levels can vary significantly. For instance, while honey might seduce the palate with its rich, floral notes, it can also cause a rapid increase in blood glucose levels, similar to that of regular sugar. The key to utilizing natural sweeteners lies in understanding their glycemic index—a measure of how quickly foods raise blood sugar levels—and integrating them judiciously into a diet that prioritizes glycemic control.

On the other side of the sweetener spectrum are artificial sweeteners, marvels of human ingenuity designed to mimic the sweetness of sugar with minimal to no calories. These include aspartame, sucralose, and saccharin, among others, each engineered to satisfy the sweet tooth without the accompanying surge in glucose levels. Their invention was a watershed moment for diabetes management, offering a way to enjoy sweet treats without the immediate metabolic repercussions of sugar.

Yet, the narrative surrounding artificial sweeteners is not without its twists and turns. While they offer undeniable benefits in terms of calorie and carbohydrate control, debates swirl around their long-term impact on health, including potential effects on appetite, gut health, and even glucose tolerance over time. The decision to incorporate artificial sweeteners into one's diet is thus not to be made lightly but with a careful consideration of both their benefits and the shadows of doubt that linger around them.

Navigating this terrain requires a nuanced understanding of both the body's response to these sweeteners and the goals of diabetes management. For someone striving to maintain stable blood sugar levels, the allure of artificial sweeteners' low glycemic impact is undeniable. However, this choice must be balanced with a consideration of the whole dietary pattern and an awareness of how artificial sweeteners fit into a holistic approach to health.

The intersection of taste preference and health necessity further complicates the choice between natural and artificial sweeteners. The ideal sweetener not only has to align with dietary management goals but also satisfy the palate. This conundrum invites a personalized approach to selecting sweeteners, one that weighs the pros and cons of each option against individual health metrics, dietary habits, and, importantly, the joy of eating.

The quest for the right sweetener, therefore, is not a one-size-fits-all journey but a personal voyage through a landscape dotted with options, each with its own merits and drawbacks. It's about finding balance—between managing diabetes and delighting in the pleasures of food, between the natural allure of sugar and the scientific marvel of artificial sweeteners. This delicate balance is where the art of dietary management meets the science of nutrition, a crossroads that demands knowledge, understanding, and a touch of culinary creativity.

In this exploration, the choice between natural and artificial sweeteners becomes more than a mere dietary decision; it's a reflection of one's approach to managing diabetes, a statement of personal health philosophy, and an expression of culinary preference. It's a decision that influences not just the glycemic outcome of a meal but the sensory experience of eating, the satisfaction of cravings, and ultimately, the quality of life. As we navigate this complex terrain, the goal remains clear: to harness the power of sweeteners in a way that supports health, brings joy to the palate, and elevates the art of cooking to new, delicious heights.

How to Choose the Right Sugar Substitute for Your Dessert

Selecting the right sugar substitute for your dessert is akin to choosing the perfect accessory for an outfit—it must complement, enhance, and complete the ensemble without overwhelming it. This decision is pivotal in the culinary realm, especially for those mindful of managing diabetes, as it can significantly affect both the taste and nutritional content of a dessert. The process of choosing the right sugar substitute isn't merely about swapping one sweetener for another; it's about understanding the chemistry of flavors, the nuances of sweetness, and the health implications tied to each option.

When venturing into the world of sugar substitutes, it's crucial to first consider the desired outcome for your dessert. Are you aiming for a rich, decadent chocolate cake, or a light, airy angel food cake? The intensity and type of sweetness can vary widely among substitutes, affecting not only the taste but also the texture and appearance of your creation. For instance, natural sweeteners like honey and maple syrup bring a moisture and depth of flavor that can enhance certain baked goods, while artificial sweeteners may offer a similar level of sweetness without the added calories or carbohydrates, but could alter the texture or mouthfeel of your dessert.

Understanding the properties of various sugar substitutes is paramount. Natural sweeteners, for instance, often contain fructose, which can impact blood sugar levels differently than glucose. They may also contribute additional calories and carbohydrates, which are important considerations for individuals managing diabetes. On the other hand, artificial sweeteners, while calorie-free, may have a more intense level of sweetness, requiring adjustments to recipes to avoid overpowering the dessert with sweetness.

The compatibility of a sugar substitute with the cooking process is another crucial aspect to consider. Some sweeteners, such as certain artificial ones, may not caramelize or react to heat in the same way as sugar, affecting the color and texture of baked goods. Additionally, the heat stability of sweeteners varies, with some losing their sweetness at high temperatures, making them unsuitable for baking or cooking.

The nutritional profile and health implications of each sugar substitute must also be carefully weighed. For individuals with diabetes, the glycemic index of a sweetener—how quickly it raises blood sugar levels—is a critical factor. While artificial sweeteners may not directly impact blood sugar levels, their long-term effects on health, appetite, and glucose tolerance are areas of ongoing research and debate. Moreover, some people may experience digestive discomfort or other adverse effects from certain sugar alcohols or artificial sweeteners, highlighting the importance of personal tolerance and preferences.

Personal taste preferences play a significant role in the selection process. The taste of sweeteners can vary dramatically, with some having a bitter aftertaste or a different sweetness profile than sugar. Experimentation is often necessary to find the substitute that best matches one's taste preferences and works well in specific recipes.

Cultural and environmental considerations may also influence the choice of sweetener. For example, sustainability-minded individuals might prefer natural sweeteners that are produced in an environmentally friendly manner, while those with specific dietary restrictions or ethical concerns may opt for sweeteners that align with their values.

Incorporating sugar substitutes into desserts is an art that requires a balance of science, creativity, and personal preference. It involves not only understanding the characteristics and impacts of each sweetener but also experimenting with proportions and combinations to achieve the desired taste and texture. This process, while potentially complex, opens up a world of possibilities for creating delightful desserts that cater to a wide range of dietary needs and preferences.

Ultimately, choosing the right sugar substitute for your dessert is a deeply personal decision that intertwines health considerations, taste preferences, and culinary goals. It's a journey of discovery, where each sweetener offers its own unique qualities and challenges. By approaching this selection process with knowledge, curiosity, and a willingness to experiment, you can unlock new dimensions of flavor and enjoyment in your desserts, transforming them into not just treats, but experiences that nourish both body and soul.

Contraindications and What to Watch Out For

As we navigate the sweet waters of sugar substitutes in our culinary endeavors, particularly in crafting desserts that delight without the added dietary concerns, we must also steer our ship with caution. The realm of sugar substitutes, both natural and artificial, is fraught with nuances and potential pitfalls that require our vigilant attention. Understanding the contraindications and what to watch out for is not just a matter of dietary preference but a crucial aspect of maintaining health and wellness, especially for individuals managing diabetes or other health conditions.

The allure of sugar substitutes is undeniable. They promise the sweetness we crave without the caloric load or blood sugar spikes associated with traditional sugar. However, this promise comes with a caveat—a need for awareness and understanding of how these substitutes interact with our bodies and affect our health.

Firstly, the impact of sugar substitutes on blood sugar levels varies widely. While many artificial sweeteners are touted for their minimal effect on blood glucose, not all substitutes are created equal. For instance, sugar alcohols such as xylitol and maltitol can still affect blood sugar levels, albeit less drastically than regular sugar. Individuals with diabetes should approach these substitutes with an informed perspective, understanding that "sugar-free" does not necessarily mean "consequence-free."

Moreover, gastrointestinal discomfort is a common concern with certain sugar substitutes. Sugar alcohols, in particular, are notorious for causing bloating, gas, and diarrhea when consumed in excess. This is due to their partial absorption in the intestine, leading to fermentation by gut bacteria. The threshold for what constitutes "excess" varies from person to person, making it important to start with small amounts and gauge individual tolerance.

The potential impact of artificial sweeteners on appetite and weight management is another area of caution. Research suggests that the consumption of artificially sweetened products may paradoxically lead to weight gain in some individuals. Theories propose that artificial sweeteners could disrupt the body's natural ability to regulate calorie intake, leading to increased hunger and subsequent overeating of other foods. While the evidence is not conclusive, this possibility warrants a mindful approach to the use of artificial sweeteners, especially for those closely monitoring their weight.

Concerns extend beyond physical health to include mental well-being. Some studies suggest a correlation between the consumption of artificial sweeteners and an increased risk of mood disorders, such as depression. Though the research is still evolving, it underscores the importance of considering the broader implications of our dietary choices on our overall health.

Moreover, the safety of long-term consumption of certain artificial sweeteners remains a topic of debate among health professionals and regulatory agencies. While many sweeteners are deemed safe for the general population, individuals with specific health conditions, such as phenylketonuria (PKU), must avoid certain artificial sweeteners like aspartame. This condition, though rare, highlights the necessity of understanding personal health conditions and the implications of various sugar substitutes.

Additionally, the environmental impact of producing and consuming certain sugar substitutes is an often-overlooked consideration. The cultivation and processing of natural sweeteners, such as stevia, can have significant environmental footprints, raising questions about the sustainability of our sweetener choices. Ethical consumers may wish to consider the broader ecological implications of their dietary preferences, seeking substitutes that align with their values of environmental stewardship.

Navigating the world of sugar substitutes, then, is not merely a culinary challenge but a holistic health consideration. It requires a judicious approach, informed by current research, personal health status, and individual body responses. Experimentation, coupled with moderation, emerges as a prudent strategy, allowing for the enjoyment of sweetness while minimizing potential adverse effects.

In conclusion, the journey through the land of sugar substitutes is one of balance and awareness. By arming ourselves with knowledge about the contraindications and being vigilant about how we incorporate these substitutes into our diets, we can enjoy the pleasures of sweet treats while safeguarding our health. This mindful approach to sweetness not only enhances our culinary experiences but also contributes to a lifestyle that prioritizes well-being and informed choice, making each dessert not just a treat for the taste buds but a testament to our commitment to health.

Chapter 2: Flour Power: Choosing the Right Flour for Diabetic Desserts

Whole Grains vs. Refined Flours: What's Best for Blood Sugar Control

In the vibrant tapestry of culinary arts, flour is not just a staple ingredient but a foundational pillar that dictates the texture, structure, and nutritional profile of our beloved desserts. For individuals managing diabetes, the choice between whole grains and refined flours is more than a culinary preference; it's a decision with profound implications for blood sugar control and overall health.

Whole grains, in their unrefined glory, retain the bran, germ, and endosperm, offering a treasure trove of nutrients, including fiber, vitamins, and minerals. This holistic composition plays a pivotal role in the management of blood sugar levels. The fiber in whole grains slows down the absorption of glucose into the bloodstream, preventing the rapid spikes that can occur with the consumption of refined flours. Moreover, the presence of essential nutrients in whole grains supports overall metabolic health, contributing to a more stable and efficient energy utilization by the body.

Refined flours, on the other hand, have been stripped of the bran and germ, leaving behind the endosperm. This process results in a product with a finer texture and longer shelf life but at the cost of nutritional bankruptcy. Without the fiber and nutrients found in whole grains, refined flours can cause a swift increase in blood sugar levels, presenting a significant challenge for individuals striving to manage their diabetes. The consumption of refined flours is often linked to a higher risk of developing type 2 diabetes, among other metabolic disorders, underscoring the importance of choosing whole grains for better blood sugar control.

The impact of flour choice extends beyond the immediate glycemic response. The long-term effects of consuming whole grains as opposed to refined flours can be profound. Studies have shown that a diet rich in whole grains is associated with a lower risk of heart disease, obesity, and certain types of cancer. For individuals with diabetes, who are at an increased risk of cardiovascular complications, incorporating whole grains into their diet can be a powerful step toward better health.

However, the transition to whole grain flours in baking requires a nuanced understanding of their properties. Whole grain flours tend to be denser and can absorb more liquid than their refined counterparts. This characteristic may necessitate adjustments in recipes, such as increasing the amount of liquid or leavening agents, to achieve the desired texture and flavor. Experimentation and patience become key ingredients in the process of adapting traditional recipes to incorporate whole grains successfully.

The variety of whole grain flours available offers a palette of flavors and textures for the adventurous baker. Beyond the familiar whole wheat flour, there are options like spelt, barley, and rye, each bringing its unique nutritional profile and taste to the table. These flours can be used alone or in combination to create desserts that are not only healthier but also richer in flavor and texture.

Yet, the choice between whole grains and refined flours is not always black and white. For individuals with gluten sensitivity or celiac disease, traditional whole grain flours may not be suitable. In such cases, gluten-free whole grains, such as quinoa, buckwheat, and amaranth, offer a viable alternative, allowing for the benefits of whole grains without the adverse effects of gluten.

In the realm of diabetic desserts, the use of whole grain flours signifies a commitment to health without the sacrifice of pleasure. The richness of flavors and textures available in whole grain flours can transform a simple dessert into a complex and satisfying experience, proving that managing diabetes through diet does not have to be a journey of deprivation.

The art of choosing the right flour for diabetic desserts is, therefore, a delicate dance between nutritional science and culinary creativity. It involves a deep appreciation for the natural bounty of whole grains and a willingness to explore and innovate within the constraints of dietary management. By prioritizing whole grains over refined flours, individuals with diabetes can enjoy a wider range of desserts that nourish the body, delight the senses, and support the journey toward better health.

In this exploration of flours, we uncover not just the impact of our choices on blood sugar levels, but also the opportunity to redefine what it means to indulge. The decision to embrace whole grains is a testament to the power of food as medicine—a philosophy that champions the integration of nutritional wisdom with culinary excellence, paving the way for a future where diabetes management is as much about enjoyment as it is about health.

Almond, Coconut, and Other Low-Carb Flour Alternatives

In the evolving landscape of diabetic-friendly baking, the exploration of low-carb flour alternatives has emerged as a culinary revolution, transforming the way we think about and create desserts. Almond, coconut, and other low-carb flours have become the keystones of this transformation, offering a way to indulge in sweets without the worry of spiking blood sugar levels. This shift toward alternative flours isn't just about maintaining dietary restrictions; it's a movement towards reimagining dessert as a part of a healthy, balanced diet for individuals managing diabetes.

Almond flour, made from finely ground almonds, is a powerhouse of nutrition, rich in protein, healthy fats, and vitamins, while being low in carbohydrates. Its subtly sweet, nutty flavor enhances baked goods with a depth of taste and a moist, tender crumb that's hard to achieve with traditional wheat flours. Beyond its taste and nutritional benefits, almond flour's low glycemic index makes it a star in the diabetic kitchen, allowing for the creation of desserts that satisfy the sweet tooth without compromising blood sugar control.

Coconut flour, another gem in the realm of low-carb baking, is crafted from dried and ground coconut meat. It's a flour that demands attention and respect, given its high fiber content and absorbent nature. Coconut flour can be tricky to work with, as it tends to require more liquid than other flours. However, when mastered, it yields baked goods that are light, fluffy, and imbued with a delicate coconut essence. Its low carbohydrate content, coupled with its high fiber, makes it an excellent choice for those looking to manage their diabetes while still enjoying rich, flavorful desserts.

The exploration of low-carb flours extends beyond almond and coconut to include other innovative alternatives such as flaxseed meal, chia flour, and even cauliflower flour. Each brings its unique nutritional profile, flavor, and baking properties to the table, expanding the possibilities for diabetic-friendly desserts. Flaxseed meal, with its earthy tone, offers a boost of omega-3 fatty acids, while chia flour introduces a subtle crunch and a dose of antioxidants. Cauliflower flour, though less common, presents a neutral base capable of taking on flavors while keeping carbs in check.

The incorporation of these low-carb flour alternatives into dessert recipes is not just a matter of substitution; it's an art that requires understanding and adaptation. The unique properties of each flour—almond's moisture, coconut's absorbency, flaxseed's density—mean that successful use often involves a dance of adjustments to other ingredients and baking times. The reward for this careful calibration is a repertoire of desserts that are not only safe for those managing diabetes but are also richer in nutrients and flavors than their traditional counterparts.

This movement towards low-carb flours is also reflective of a broader shift in our understanding of health and wellness. It challenges the conventional wisdom that desserts are inherently unhealthy, presenting an alternative narrative where sweets can be both a delight to the senses and a contribution to our health. For individuals with diabetes, this shift is particularly empowering, offering a way to celebrate life's sweet moments without fear of disrupting blood sugar balance.

Moreover, the rise of low-carb flour alternatives speaks to a growing recognition of the importance of dietary customization. What works for one individual may not work for another, making the variety of available flours not just a culinary luxury but a necessity. By experimenting with different flours, individuals can find the combination that best suits their dietary needs, taste preferences, and baking style, crafting desserts that are uniquely theirs.

In embracing almond, coconut, and other low-carb flours, we're not just adapting recipes; we're redefining what it means to bake and enjoy desserts within a diabetic-friendly framework. This redefinition is not merely about avoiding high-carb ingredients; it's about creating something new, something that stands on its own merits of taste, texture, and nutritional value. It's a testament to the creativity and resilience of those managing diabetes, who seek not just to live with their condition but to thrive despite it.

As we continue to explore and expand the boundaries of diabetic-friendly baking, almond, coconut, and other low-carb flour alternatives stand as beacons of innovation and hope. They represent not just a shift in ingredients but a transformation in the way we think about food, health, and pleasure. In this new era of baking, desserts are no longer seen as guilty pleasures but as celebrations of life, crafted with care, creativity, and an eye towards health.

Gluten-Free Baking for Diabetics

In the contemporary culinary landscape, gluten-free baking stands not just as a trend, but as a necessity for many. For individuals with diabetes, especially those also dealing with gluten sensitivity or celiac disease, navigating the world of desserts can feel like moving through a minefield. Gluten-free baking for diabetics is more than a dietary restriction; it's an art form that marries health with indulgence, ensuring that every bite is both safe and sumptuously satisfying. The cornerstone of gluten-free baking lies in the flour—or rather, the innovative alternatives to traditional wheat flour. These alternatives are not merely substitutes but are ingredients that bring their unique flavors, textures, and nutritional profiles to the table, transforming gluten-free baking from a challenge into an exploration of taste and health.

Navigating this realm requires an understanding of how gluten, the protein found in wheat, barley, and rye, affects both the body and the baking process. Gluten's elasticity and ability to trap air make it instrumental in achieving the light, airy textures of many classic baked goods. However, for those whose bodies rebel against gluten, the quest becomes finding flour alternatives that can mimic these qualities without the adverse health effects.

The variety of gluten-free flours available today is a testament to culinary innovation. Almond flour, with its rich, nutty flavor, offers a high-protein, low-carbohydrate alternative that is especially beneficial for diabetics monitoring their blood sugar levels. Its high fat content lends moisture to baked goods, making it an excellent choice for tender cakes and cookies. Coconut flour, another staple in the gluten-free pantry, is highly absorbent and rich in fiber, requiring adjustments in liquid ratios in recipes but resulting in baked goods that help manage blood sugar spikes.

Beyond almond and coconut flour, a plethora of other gluten-free flours offer a canvas for culinary creativity. Flours made from ancient grains like quinoa and amaranth not only provide the structural backbone for gluten-free baking but also contribute a variety of nutrients, including protein, fiber, and essential minerals, supporting overall health in addition to blood sugar control.

However, gluten-free baking for diabetics is not without its challenges. The absence of gluten means that other ingredients must often be enlisted to provide structure and volume to baked goods. Xanthan gum and guar gum are frequently used as binders in gluten-free baking, mimicking gluten's elastic properties. The balance of these ingredients is crucial; too little, and baked goods may crumble, too much, and they may become gummy. Mastering this balance is part of the art of gluten-free baking, requiring patience and practice.

Moreover, the glycemic index of gluten-free flours varies, necessitating mindful selection to manage blood sugar levels effectively. While some gluten-free flours offer the benefit of lower carbohydrate content, others, particularly those made from starchy grains or tubers, can have a higher glycemic index than their wheat counterparts. Choosing flours with a lower glycemic index and combining them with other low-glycemic ingredients can help create desserts that are both delicious and diabetes-friendly.

Creating a gluten-free dessert that delights the palate involves more than simply substituting one flour for another. It's about understanding the unique properties of each flour alternative and how they interact with other ingredients. It's an exploration of flavor, where the absence of gluten opens the door to a world of diverse and delicious possibilities.

For those managing diabetes, gluten-free baking becomes a harmonious blend of nutritional science and culinary art. It's a pathway to enjoying the sweeter things in life without compromising health or flavor. The process of selecting, combining, and experimenting with gluten-free flours and other ingredients not only results in delectable desserts but also empowers individuals to take control of their health and wellbeing.

In essence, gluten-free baking for diabetics is a testament to the resilience and creativity of the human spirit. It's a celebration of diversity in both ingredients and individuals, recognizing that with the right knowledge and approach, limitations can be transformed into opportunities. Through the lens of gluten-free baking, we see not just a dietary need, but a culinary adventure that invites all to the table to share in the joy of delicious, health-conscious desserts.

Chapter 3: Cakes & Cupcakes for Every Occasion

Low-Carb Sponge Cake Basics

Recipe 1: Vanilla Almond Sponge Cake

P.T.: 35 minutes

Ingr.: 1 cup almond flour, 4 eggs (separated), 1/3 cup erythritol, 1 tsp vanilla extract, 1/4 tsp cream of tartar, pinch of salt

M.C.: Oven-baked

Procedure: Beat egg whites with cream of tartar until stiff peaks form. In another bowl, mix egg yolks, erythritol, and vanilla. Fold in almond flour and salt, then gently fold in egg whites. Bake at 350°F for 25 minutes.

N.V.: Calories: 160, Net Carbs: 2g, Fat: 14g, Protein: 6g

Recipe 2: Lemon Zest Sponge Cake

P.T.: 40 minutes

Ingr.: 1 cup coconut flour, 5 eggs (separated), zest of 1 lemon, 1/2 cup monk fruit sweetener, 1 tsp lemon extract, 1/2 tsp baking powder

M.C.: Oven-baked

Procedure: Whisk egg yolks, lemon zest, lemon extract, and monk fruit. In a separate bowl, beat egg whites to stiff peaks. Fold egg whites into yolk mixture with coconut flour and baking powder. Pour into pan and bake at 325°F for 30 minutes.

N.V.: Calories: 120, Net Carbs: 3g, Fat: 9g, Protein: 4g

Recipe 3: Chocolate Hazelnut Sponge Cake

P.T.: 45 minutes

Ingr.: 1 cup hazelnut meal, 4 eggs, 1/3 cup cocoa powder, 1/2 cup erythritol, 1 tsp vanilla, 1/4 tsp sea salt

M.C.: Oven-baked

Procedure: Separate eggs. Mix yolks with erythritol, vanilla, cocoa, and hazelnut meal. Beat whites to peaks, fold into mix. Bake at 340°F for 25 mins.

N.V.: Calories: 175, Net Carbs: 3g, Fat: 15g, Protein: 7g

Recipe 4: Cinnamon Apple Sponge Cake

P.T.: 50 minutes

Ingr.: 2 cups almond flour, 4 eggs (separated), 1/2 cup grated apple, 1/4 cup erythritol, 1 tsp cinnamon, 1/2 tsp nutmeg, 1 tsp baking powder

M.C.: Oven-baked

Procedure: Beat yolks with erythritol, cinnamon, nutmeg, and apple. Whisk whites to stiff peaks. Fold whites into yolk mix with almond flour. Bake at 350°F for 30 mins.

N.V.: Calories: 165, Net Carbs: 4g, Fat: 13g, Protein: 6g

Recipe 5: Coconut Lime Sponge Cake

P.T.: 38 minutes

Ingr.: 1 cup coconut flour, zest of 1 lime, 4 eggs (separated), 1/2 cup erythritol, 1 tsp lime juice, 1/4 tsp salt

M.C.: Oven-baked

Procedure: Beat yolks with erythritol, lime zest, and juice. In another bowl, beat whites with salt to peaks. Fold in coconut flour and whites. Bake at 340°F for 28 mins.

N.V.: Calories: 130, Net Carbs: 3g, Fat: 10g, Protein: 5g

Recipe 6: Pumpkin Spice Sponge Cake

P.T.: 42 minutes

Ingr.: 1 cup almond flour, 1/2 cup pumpkin puree, 5 eggs (separated), 1/3 cup erythritol, 1 tsp pumpkin spice, 1/2 tsp baking powder

M.C.: Oven-baked

Procedure: Mix egg yolks, pumpkin puree, erythritol, and spice. Beat whites to peaks, fold into pumpkin mixture with flour. Bake at 350°F for 30 mins.

N.V.: Calories: 150, Net Carbs: 4g, Fat: 11g, Protein: 6g

Decorating Diabetic-Friendly Cakes

Recipe 1: Vanilla Bean Cream Cheese Frosting

P.T.: 15 minutes

Ingr:

1 cup of cream cheese, softened

1/4 cup unsalted butter, softened

1/4 cup erythritol, powdered

1 vanilla bean, scraped

1 tsp vanilla extract

2-3 tbsp unsweetened almond milk

M.C.: Mixing

Procedure:

In a medium bowl, beat the cream cheese and butter together until smooth.

Gradually add powdered erythritol, vanilla bean seeds, and vanilla extract, beating until well combined.

Thin the frosting with almond milk to desired consistency, beating until fluffy.

N.V.: Calories: 120, Fat: 12g, Carbs: 2g, Protein: 2g, Sugar: 1g.

Recipe 2: Chocolate Avocado Ganache

P.T.: 10 minutes

Ingr:

2 ripe avocados, peeled and pitted

1/2 cup unsweetened cocoa powder

1/4 cup almond milk

1/3 cup monk fruit sweetener

1 tsp vanilla extract

M.C.: Blending

Procedure:

Blend avocados, cocoa powder, almond milk, monk fruit sweetener, and vanilla extract until smooth.

Refrigerate for 30 minutes until thickened.

Spread over cakes or cupcakes as desired.

N.V.: Calories: 98, Fat: 7g, Carbs: 8g, Fiber: 5g, Protein: 2g.

Recipe 3: Berry Compote Topping

P.T.: 20 minutes

Ingr:

2 cups mixed berries (strawberries, blueberries, raspberries)

1/4 cup water

2 tbsp chia seeds

1/4 cup erythritol

M.C.: Simmering

Procedure:

In a saucepan, combine berries, water, and erythritol. Simmer over medium heat for 10 minutes.

Stir in chia seeds and cook for another 5

minutes until thickened.

Cool before spreading on cakes.

N.V.: Calories: 50, Fat: 1g, Carbs: 11g, Fiber: 4g, Protein: 1g.

Recipe 4: Almond Crunch Topping

P.T.: 15 minutes

Ingr:

1/2 cup sliced almonds

2 tbsp unsalted butter

1 tbsp erythritol

Pinch of salt

M.C.: Toasting

Procedure:

Melt butter in a skillet over medium heat.

Add almonds, erythritol, and salt, cooking until golden and caramelized.

Cool before using as a cake topping.

N.V.: Calories: 80, Fat: 7g, Carbs: 2g, Protein: 2g.

Recipe 5: Coconut Cream Frosting

P.T.: 10 minutes + chilling

Ingr:

1 can (14 oz) full-fat coconut milk, chilled overnight

1/4 cup erythritol, powdered

1 tsp vanilla extract

M.C.: Whipping

Procedure:

Scoop the solid coconut cream into a bowl, leaving the liquid behind.

Beat with powdered erythritol and vanilla until creamy and smooth.

Chill until ready to use.

N.V.: Calories: 100, Fat: 10g, Carbs: 3g, Protein: 1g.

Recipe 6: Lemon Zest Glaze

P.T.: 10 minutes

Ingr:

1/4 cup fresh lemon juice

1 tsp lemon zest

1/4 cup erythritol, powdered

2 tbsp water

M.C.: Mixing

Procedure:

Whisk together lemon juice, lemon zest, powdered erythritol, and water until smooth.

Drizzle over cakes or cupcakes for a tangy finish.

N.V.: Negligible fats and proteins, Carbs: 1g.

Recipe 7: Sugar-Free Sprinkles

P.T.: 1 hour + drying

Ingr:

1/4 cup erythritol, granulated

Natural food coloring

1 tsp cornstarch (optional, for texture)

M.C.: Drying

Procedure:

Divide erythritol into small bowls, adding a drop of food coloring to each and mixing well.

Spread colored erythritol on a baking sheet and let dry for 1 hour.

Pulse in a blender if a finer texture is desired. Use as sprinkles.

N.V.: Minimal calories, Fat: 0g, Carbs: 0g.

Special Occasion Showstoppers

Recipe 1: Triple Berry Layer Cake

P.T.: 1 hour 30 minutes

Ingr:

For Cake: Almond flour, erythritol, eggs, unsalted butter, vanilla extract, baking powder.

For Filling: Mixed berries (strawberries, raspberries, blueberries), chia seeds, monk fruit sweetener.

For Frosting: Cream cheese, heavy cream, powdered erythritol, lemon zest.

M.C.: Baking and mixing

Procedure:

Bake almond flour-based sponge cakes flavored with vanilla and erythritol.

Simmer berries with monk fruit sweetener and chia seeds to make a jam-like filling.

Whip cream cheese, heavy cream, powdered erythritol, and lemon zest for frosting.

Assemble the cake with layers of sponge, berry filling, and frosting.

N.V.: Estimated per serving: Calories: 320, Fat: 28g, Carbs: 10g (net), Protein: 8g.

Recipe 2: Chocolate-Hazelnut Torte

P.T.: 1 hour

Ingr:

For Torte: Hazelnut flour, cocoa powder, eggs, unsalted butter, erythritol, espresso powder.

For Ganache: Dark chocolate (sugar-free), heavy cream, vanilla extract.

M.C.: Baking and boiling

Procedure:

Mix hazelnut flour, cocoa, and erythritol; add wet ingredients to form batter.

Bake until set; cool completely.

Heat cream for ganache, pour over chocolate, add vanilla, and stir until smooth.

Glaze torte with ganache.

N.V.: Estimated per serving: Calories: 290, Fat: 25g, Carbs: 5g (net), Protein: 6g.

Recipe 3: Lemon Almond Pavlova

P.T.: 2 hours

Ingr:

For Pavlova: Egg whites, cream of tartar, powdered erythritol, almond extract.

For Topping: Whipped cream (sugar-free), fresh raspberries, lemon zest.

M.C.: Baking and whipping

Procedure:

Whip egg whites with cream of tartar and erythritol to stiff peaks, fold in almond extract.

Shape into a disk and bake at low temp until crisp on the outside.

Top with sugar-free whipped cream, raspberries, and lemon zest before serving.

N.V.: Estimated per serving: Calories: 90, Fat: 7g, Carbs: 3g (net), Protein: 4g.

Recipe 4: Decadent Flourless Chocolate Cake

P.T.: 45 minutes

Ingr:

Dark chocolate (sugar-free), unsalted butter, erythritol, eggs, vanilla extract, salt.

M.C.: Baking

Procedure:

Melt chocolate and butter, stir in erythritol and vanilla.

Beat in eggs one at a time, pour into pan, and bake.

Serve with a dusting of cocoa powder or sugar-free powdered sugar.

N.V.: Estimated per serving: Calories: 300, Fat: 28g, Carbs: 5g (net), Protein: 6g.

Recipe 5: Vanilla Bean Cheesecake with Almond Crust

P.T.: 1 hour + chilling

Ingr:

For Crust: Almond flour, melted butter, erythritol.

For Filling: Cream cheese, sour cream, eggs, vanilla bean, powdered erythritol.

M.C.: Baking

Procedure:

Mix almond flour with butter and erythritol, press into pan, bake briefly.

Blend filling ingredients, pour over crust, bake until set.

Chill overnight; serve with fresh berries.

N.V.: Estimated per serving: Calories: 320, Fat: 30g, Carbs: 6g (net), Protein: 7g.

Recipe 6: Red Velvet Cupcakes with Cream Cheese Frosting

P.T.: 30 minutes + baking

Ingr:

For Cupcakes: Almond flour, cocoa powder, beet powder (for color), eggs, unsalted butter, erythritol.

For Frosting: Cream cheese, butter,

powdered erythritol, vanilla extract.

M.C.: Baking and mixing

Procedure:

Combine dry ingredients, mix in wet ingredients, divide into cupcake liners, and bake.

Whip frosting ingredients together until smooth; frost cupcakes once cooled.

N.V.: Estimated per serving: Calories: 200, Fat: 18g, Carbs: 4g (net), Protein: 5g.

Recipe 7: Pear and Ginger Spice Cake

P.T.: 1 hour

Ingr:

For Cake: Almond flour, grated ginger, cinnamon, nutmeg, erythritol, eggs, grated pear, unsalted butter.

For Glaze: Cream cheese, powdered erythritol, lemon juice, grated ginger.

M.C.: Baking and blending

Procedure:

Mix dry ingredients, incorporate wet ingredients including grated pear.

Bake until a toothpick comes out clean.

Blend glaze ingredients; drizzle over cooled cake.

N.V.: Estimated per serving: Calories: 250, Fat: 22g, Carbs: 8g (net), Protein: 6g.

Chapter 4: Cookies & Bars for Easy Snacking

Crunchy and Crispy

Recipe 1: Almond Flour Sesame Crackers

P.T.: 25 minutes

Ingr:

2 cups almond flour

1 tbsp ground flaxseed

3 tbsp sesame seeds

1/2 tsp salt

1 large egg

2 tbsp olive oil

M.C.: Baking

Procedure:

Preheat oven to 350°F (175°C).

Mix almond flour, flaxseed, sesame seeds, and salt in a bowl.

Whisk egg and olive oil together; combine with dry ingredients to form a dough.

Roll out dough between two pieces of parchment paper to 1/8 inch thickness.

Cut into squares, transfer to a baking sheet, and bake for 12-15 minutes until golden.

N.V.: Calories: 160, Fat: 14g, Carbs: 4g (net), Protein: 6g.

Recipe 2: Crunchy Peanut Butter Cookies

P.T.: 20 minutes

Ingr:

1 cup natural peanut butter (unsweetened)

1/2 cup erythritol

1 egg

1 tsp vanilla extract

1/2 tsp baking soda

M.C.: Baking

Procedure:

Preheat oven to 350°F (175°C).

Mix all ingredients in a bowl until well combined.

Scoop tablespoonfuls of dough, roll into balls, and place on a baking sheet.

Flatten each ball with a fork, making a crisscross pattern.

Bake for 10-12 minutes until edges are golden.

N.V.: Calories: 120, Fat: 10g, Carbs: 3g (net), Protein: 5g.

Recipe 3: Cheddar Almond Flour Crackers

P.T.: 30 minutes

Ingr:

1 1/2 cups almond flour

1 cup grated sharp cheddar cheese

1/4 tsp cayenne pepper

1/4 tsp garlic powder

1/4 cup unsalted butter, melted

M.C.: Baking

Procedure:

Preheat oven to 350°F (175°C).

Combine almond flour, cheese, cayenne, and garlic powder in a bowl.

Mix in melted butter until a dough forms.

Roll out dough to 1/8 inch thickness and cut into squares.

Bake for 15-17 minutes until crispy and golden.

N.V.: Calories: 150, Fat: 12g, Carbs: 2g (net), Protein: 7g.

Recipe 4: Cinnamon Pecan Brittle

P.T.: 15 minutes + cooling

Ingr:

1 cup chopped pecans

1/4 cup erythritol

1 tsp cinnamon

1 egg white

Pinch of salt

M.C.: Baking

Procedure:

Preheat oven to 300°F (150°C).

Whip egg white to soft peaks, fold in erythritol, cinnamon, and salt.

Gently fold in chopped pecans until well coated.

Spread mixture thinly on a parchment-lined baking sheet.

Bake for 20 minutes, let cool until brittle.

N.V.: Calories: 140, Fat: 13g, Carbs: 3g (net), Protein: 2g.

Recipe 5: Coconut Crisps

P.T.: 15 minutes

Ingr:

2 cups unsweetened shredded coconut

1/4 cup erythritol

2 egg whites

1 tsp vanilla extract

M.C.: Baking

Procedure:

Preheat oven to 325°F (163°C).

Mix all ingredients in a bowl until well combined.

Drop spoonfuls onto a baking sheet lined with parchment paper, flattening slightly.

Bake for 12-15 minutes until edges are golden brown.

N.V.: Calories: 100, Fat: 9g, Carbs: 2g (net), Protein: 2g.

Recipe 6: Parmesan Rosemary Crisps

P.T.: 10 minutes

Ingr:

1 cup grated Parmesan cheese

1 tbsp finely chopped fresh rosemary

1/2 tsp black pepper

M.C.: Baking

Procedure:

Preheat oven to 400°F (200°C).

Mix Parmesan, rosemary, and pepper in a bowl.

Spoon tablespoonfuls of the mixture onto a baking sheet lined with parchment, spreading into thin circles.

Bake for 5-7 minutes until golden and crisp.

N.V.: Calories: 110, Fat: 7g, Carbs: 1g (net), Protein: 10g.

Recipe 7: Spicy Pumpkin Seeds

P.T.: 25 minutes

Ingr:

1 cup raw pumpkin seeds

1 tbsp olive oil

1/2 tsp chili powder

1/4 tsp cumin

Salt to taste

M.C.: Roasting

Procedure:

Preheat oven to 375°F (190°C).

Toss pumpkin seeds with olive oil, chili powder, cumin, and salt.

Spread on a baking sheet in a single layer.

Roast for 15-20 minutes, stirring occasionally, until crispy.

N.V.: Calories: 150, Fat: 13g, Carbs: 3g (net), Protein: 7g.

Soft and Chewy Bars for Energy Boosts

Recipe 1: No-Bake Peanut Butter Chocolate Chip Bars

P.T.: 15 minutes + chilling

Ingr:

1 cup natural peanut butter (unsweetened)

1/4 cup coconut oil

1/4 cup erythritol (powdered)

1/2 cup almond flour

1/4 cup sugar-free chocolate chips

1 tsp vanilla extract

M.C.: No-bake

Procedure:

Melt peanut butter and coconut oil together, stir in erythritol and vanilla extract.

Mix in almond flour until well combined, then fold in chocolate chips.

Press mixture into a lined baking dish and refrigerate until set.

N.V.: Calories: 200, Fat: 16g, Carbs: 6g (net), Protein: 6g.

Recipe 2: Chewy Almond Joy Bars

P.T.: 20 minutes + chilling

Ingr:

1 cup unsweetened shredded coconut

1/2 cup almond butter

1/3 cup coconut oil

1/4 cup erythritol (powdered)

1/4 cup chopped almonds

1/4 cup sugar-free chocolate chips

M.C.: No-bake

Procedure:

Combine shredded coconut, almond butter, and coconut oil, heat slightly until mixable.

Stir in erythritol, almonds, and chocolate chips.

Press into a lined pan and chill until firm before slicing.

N.V.: Calories: 210, Fat: 18g, Carbs: 5g (net), Protein: 4g.

Recipe 3: Pumpkin Spice Protein Bars

P.T.: 15 minutes + chilling

Ingr:

1 cup pumpkin puree

1/2 cup vanilla whey protein powder (sugar-free)

1/4 cup almond flour

2 tbsp almond butter

2 tsp pumpkin pie spice

1/4 cup erythritol (powdered)

M.C.: No-bake

Procedure:

Mix all ingredients in a bowl until thoroughly combined.

Press mixture into a lined baking dish.

Chill in the fridge until set, then cut into bars.

N.V.: Calories: 100, Fat: 5g, Carbs: 4g (net), Protein: 10g.

Recipe 4: Lemon Cashew Energy Bars

P.T.: 20 minutes + chilling

Ingr:

1 cup cashews

1/2 cup unsweetened shredded coconut

1/4 cup coconut oil

1/4 cup lemon juice

Zest of 1 lemon

1/4 cup erythritol (powdered)

M.C.: No-bake

Procedure:

Blend cashews and coconut in a food processor until fine.

Add coconut oil, lemon juice, zest, and erythritol; blend until sticky.

Press into a pan and chill until firm.

N.V.: Calories: 180, Fat: 14g, Carbs: 7g (net), Protein: 4g.

Recipe 5: Cinnamon Roll Protein Bars

P.T.: 20 minutes + chilling

Ingr:

1 cup vanilla whey protein powder (sugar-free)

1/2 cup ground flaxseed

1/4 cup unsweetened almond milk

2 tbsp melted coconut oil

1 tsp cinnamon

1/4 cup erythritol (powdered)

Optional: Cream cheese frosting (sugar-free)

M.C.: No-bake

Procedure:

Mix protein powder, flaxseed, almond milk, coconut oil, cinnamon, and erythritol.

Press mixture into a lined dish, chill until set.

Top with optional cream cheese frosting before serving.

N.V.: Calories: 150, Fat: 8g, Carbs: 3g (net), Protein: 15g.

Recipe 6: Berry Bliss Granola Bars

P.T.: 20 minutes + baking

Ingr:

1 cup mixed nuts, chopped

1/2 cup unsweetened dried berries

1/4 cup chia seeds

1/4 cup flaxseed meal

1/2 cup unsweetened almond butter

1/4 cup erythritol (powdered)

1 egg white

M.C.: Baking

Procedure:

Mix nuts, berries, chia seeds, and flaxseed meal.

Warm almond butter, stir in erythritol, mix with dry ingredients, then add egg white.

Press into a lined baking dish, bake at 350°F (175°C) for 20 minutes.

N.V.: Calories: 180, Fat: 14g, Carbs: 8g (net), Protein: 6g.

Recipe 7: Dark Chocolate Mint Protein Bars

P.T.: 15 minutes + chilling

Ingr:

1 cup chocolate whey protein powder (sugar-free)

1/4 cup unsweetened cocoa powder

1/4 cup almond flour

1/4 cup coconut oil, melted

1/2 cup water

1 tsp peppermint extract

1/4 cup erythritol (powdered)

M.C.: No-bake

Procedure:

Mix all dry ingredients in a large bowl.

Combine coconut oil, water, and peppermint extract, then mix into dry ingredients.

Press into a lined pan, chill until set, then slice into bars.

N.V.: Calories: 160, Fat: 9g, Carbs: 5g (net), Protein: 15g.

No-Bake Cookies and Bars

Recipe 1: Cocoa Almond Protein Balls

P.T.: 15 minutes

Ingr:

1 cup almond butter (unsweetened)

1/4 cup cocoa powder (unsweetened)

1/2 cup coconut flour

1/4 cup sugar-free maple syrup or liquid stevia to taste

1 scoop whey protein powder (sugar-free, chocolate or vanilla)

Optional: unsweetened shredded coconut or crushed almonds for coating

M.C.: Mixing

Procedure:

In a bowl, mix almond butter, cocoa powder, coconut flour, sweetener, and protein powder until well combined.

Roll the mixture into small balls.

Optionally roll each ball in shredded coconut or crushed almonds.

Refrigerate for at least 30 minutes before serving.

N.V.: Calories: 150, Fat: 11g, Carbs: 6g (net), Protein: 7g.

Recipe 2: Lemon Cashew Coconut Bars

P.T.: 20 minutes + chilling

Ingr:

1 cup cashews (soaked for 4 hours then drained)

1 cup unsweetened shredded coconut

1/4 cup coconut oil, melted

1/4 cup sugar-free liquid sweetener

Zest and juice of 1 lemon

M.C.: Blending

Procedure:

Blend cashews, shredded coconut, coconut oil, sweetener, lemon zest, and juice until smooth.

Press the mixture into a lined square dish.

Chill in the refrigerator until firm, then cut into bars.

N.V.: Calories: 200, Fat: 16g, Carbs: 8g (net), Protein: 4g.

Recipe 3: Peanut Butter Hemp Seed Cookies

P.T.: 10 minutes

Ingr:

1/2 cup natural peanut butter (unsweetened)

1/4 cup hemp seeds

1/4 cup flaxseed meal

1/4 cup erythritol (granulated)

1 tsp vanilla extract

M.C.: Mixing

Procedure:

Mix all ingredients in a bowl until well combined.

Form the mixture into small cookies and place on a lined tray.

Chill in the refrigerator until set.

N.V.: Calories: 130, Fat: 10g, Carbs: 3g (net), Protein: 6g.

Recipe 4: Berry Bliss Bars

P.T.: 20 minutes + freezing

Ingr:

1 cup mixed berries (fresh or thawed from frozen)

1 cup unsweetened shredded coconut

1/2 cup almonds

1/4 cup chia seeds

1/4 cup coconut oil, melted

1/4 cup sugar-free syrup or liquid stevia to taste

M.C.: Blending and freezing

Procedure:

Blend all ingredients until the mixture sticks together.

Press the mixture into a lined dish.

Freeze until solid, then cut into bars.

N.V.: Calories: 180, Fat: 14g, Carbs: 7g (net), Protein: 4g.

Recipe 5: No-Bake Chocolate Walnut Brownies

P.T.: 15 minutes + chilling

Ingr:

1 cup walnuts

1 cup dates (pitted)

1/2 cup cocoa powder (unsweetened)

1/2 tsp sea salt

1/4 cup sugar-free chocolate chips (optional)

M.C.: Processing and chilling

Procedure:

Process walnuts, dates, cocoa powder, and sea salt in a food processor until the mixture begins to stick together.

Stir in chocolate chips if using.

Press into a lined square dish and chill in the refrigerator before cutting into squares.

N.V.: Calories: 160, Fat: 10g, Carbs: 8g (net), Protein: 3g.

Recipe 6: Matcha Green Tea Energy Squares

P.T.: 15 minutes + chilling

Ingr:

1 cup unsweetened shredded coconut

1/2 cup almond flour

1/4 cup coconut oil, melted

1/4 cup sugar-free syrup

2 tbsp matcha green tea powder

1 tsp vanilla extract

M.C.: Mixing

Procedure:

Mix all ingredients until well combined.

Press the mixture into a lined dish.

Chill until firm, then cut into squares.

N.V.: Calories: 190, Fat: 17g, Carbs: 5g (net), Protein: 3g.

Recipe 7: Spiced Pumpkin Seed and Nut Bars

P.T.: 20 minutes + chilling

Ingr:

1/2 cup pumpkin seeds

1/2 cup sunflower seeds

1/2 cup almonds, chopped

1/4 cup flaxseed meal

1/2 tsp cinnamon

1/4 tsp nutmeg

1/4 cup coconut oil, melted

1/4 cup sugar-free syrup or liquid stevia to taste

M.C.: Mixing

Procedure:

Mix seeds, nuts, flaxseed meal, cinnamon, and nutmeg.

Stir in melted coconut oil and sweetener.

Press into a lined dish, chill until firm, then slice.

N.V.: Calories: 180, Fat: 15g, Carbs: 6g (net), Protein: 5g.

Chapter 5: Pies & Tarts That Please Every Palate

Savory Pies for Any Meal

Recipe 1: Mediterranean Vegetable Quiche

P.T.: 45 minutes

Ingr:

For the crust: 1 1/2 cups almond flour, 1/4 cup coconut oil, 1 egg, pinch of salt.

For the filling: 1 zucchini (sliced), 1/2 cup cherry tomatoes (halved), 1/4 cup feta cheese (crumbled), 4 eggs, 1/4 cup almond milk, 1 tsp dried oregano, salt, and pepper to taste.

M.C.: Baking

Procedure:

Preheat the oven to 350°F (175°C).

Mix crust ingredients and press into a pie dish. Bake for 10 minutes.

Sauté zucchini until slightly tender. Arrange zucchini, tomatoes, and feta in the crust.

Whisk eggs, almond milk, oregano, salt, and pepper. Pour over vegetables.

Bake for 30 minutes or until the filling is set.

N.V.: Calories: 220, Fat: 18g, Carbs: 6g (net), Protein: 10g.

Recipe 2: Spinach and Mushroom Breakfast Pie

P.T.: 40 minutes

Ingr:

For the crust: 2 cups cauliflower rice, 1 egg, 1/2 cup shredded mozzarella, salt.

For the filling: 1 cup spinach (chopped), 1 cup mushrooms (sliced), 4 eggs, 1/2 cup heavy cream, 1/4 cup grated Parmesan, salt, and pepper to taste.

M.C.: Baking

Procedure:

Preheat oven to 375°F (190°C).

Combine crust ingredients, press into a pie dish, and bake for 15 minutes.

Sauté spinach and mushrooms. Spread over crust.

Mix eggs, cream, Parmesan, salt, and pepper. Pour over vegetables.

Bake for 25 minutes or until the filling is set.

N.V.: Calories: 250, Fat: 20g, Carbs: 5g (net), Protein: 12g.

Recipe 3: Low-Carb Chicken Pot Pie

P.T.: 1 hour

Ingr:

For the crust: 1 1/2 cups almond flour, 1/3 cup coconut flour, 1/2 cup butter (cold, diced), 1 egg, salt.

For the filling: 2 cups cooked chicken (shredded), 1/2 cup green peas (frozen), 1/2 cup carrots (diced), 1/2 cup celery (diced), 1 cup chicken broth (low sodium), 1/2 cup heavy cream, 1 tsp thyme, salt, and pepper.

M.C.: Baking

Procedure:

Preheat oven to 400°F (200°C).

Prepare crust dough, chill, then roll out and fit into a pie dish.

For filling, sauté carrots and celery, add chicken, peas, broth, cream, thyme, salt, and pepper. Simmer until thickened.

Fill crust with chicken mixture. Cover with a top crust layer. Bake for 30 minutes.

N.V.: Calories: 330, Fat: 25g, Carbs: 8g

(net), Protein: 18g.

Recipe 4: Cheesy Broccoli Bacon Quiche

P.T.: 50 minutes

Ingr:

For the crust: 1 3/4 cups almond flour, 1/4 cup butter (melted), salt.

For the filling: 1 cup broccoli (chopped), 1/2 cup bacon (cooked, chopped), 4 eggs, 1 cup cheddar cheese (shredded), 1/2 cup sour cream, salt, and pepper.

M.C.: Baking

Procedure:

Mix crust ingredients, press into pie dish, bake for 10 minutes at 350°F (175°C).

Steam broccoli until just tender.

Layer broccoli, bacon, and cheese in crust.

Whisk eggs, sour cream, salt, and pepper. Pour over fillings.

Bake for 35 minutes until set.

N.V.: Calories: 280, Fat: 23g, Carbs: 6g (net), Protein: 14g.

Recipe 5: Savory Turkey and Veggie Tart

P.T.: 30 minutes

Ingr:

For the crust: 1 cup almond flour, 3 tbsp coconut oil, 1 egg, salt.

For the filling: 1 cup cooked turkey (diced),

1/2 cup bell peppers (diced), 1/4 cup onions (diced), 4 eggs, 1/4 cup almond milk, 1 tsp garlic powder, salt, and pepper.

M.C.: Baking

Procedure:

Preheat oven to 375°F (190°C).

Prepare the crust and press into a tart pan. Pre-bake for 8 minutes.

Mix turkey, bell peppers, and onions. Whisk eggs, almond milk, garlic powder, salt, and pepper.

Combine egg mixture with turkey and veggies, pour into crust. Bake for 22 minutes.

N.V.: Calories: 240, Fat: 18g, Carbs: 7g (net), Protein: 15g.

Recipe 6: Beef and Mushroom Shepherd's Pie

P.T.: 1 hour

Ingr:

For the crust: Mashed cauliflower (2 cups cauliflower florets, 1/4 cup heavy cream, 2 tbsp butter, salt, and pepper).

For the filling: 1 lb ground beef, 1 cup mushrooms (sliced), 1/2 cup onions (diced), 1/2 cup beef broth (low sodium), 1 tsp rosemary, salt, and pepper.

M.C.: Baking

Procedure:

Cook cauliflower, mash with cream, butter, salt, and pepper.

Brown beef with onions and mushrooms, add broth and rosemary, simmer until thick.

Place beef mixture in a baking dish, top with mashed cauliflower. Bake at 375°F (190°C) for 25 minutes.

N.V.: Calories: 310, Fat: 22g, Carbs: 8g (net), Protein: 20g.

Recipe 7: Zucchini and Tomato Tart with Mozzarella

P.T.: 40 minutes

Ingr:

For the crust: 1 1/2 cups almond flour, 1/4 cup olive oil, 1 egg, salt.

For the filling: 1 zucchini (thinly sliced), 1 tomato (thinly sliced), 1/2 cup mozzarella cheese (sliced or shredded), 2 eggs, 1/4 cup almond milk, 1/2 tsp basil, salt, and pepper.

M.C.: Baking

Procedure:

Mix crust ingredients, press into a tart pan, bake for 10 minutes at 350°F (175°C).

Arrange zucchini, tomato, and mozzarella in the crust.

Whisk eggs, almond milk, basil, salt, and pepper. Pour over vegetables.

Bake for 30 minutes until the egg mixture is set.

N.V.: Calories: 270, Fat: 21g, Carbs: 9g (net), Protein: 12g.

Sweet and Fruity Tart Makeovers

Recipe 1: Berry Bliss Tart

P.T.: 30 minutes + chilling

Ingr:

For the crust: 1 1/2 cups almond flour, 1/4 cup coconut oil (melted), 2 tbsp erythritol.

For the filling: 1 cup mixed berries (raspberries, blueberries, strawberries), 1/2 cup sugar-free vanilla yogurt, 1 tbsp chia seeds (for thickening).

M.C.: No-bake

Procedure:

Mix almond flour, coconut oil, and erythritol; press into a tart pan; chill.

Blend half the berries with yogurt and chia seeds; spread over crust.

Top with remaining berries; chill until set.

N.V.: Calories: 180, Fat: 14g, Carbs: 8g (net), Protein: 5g.

Recipe 2: Lemon Almond Tart

P.T.: 35 minutes + chilling

Ingr:

For the crust: 2 cups almond flour, 1/3 cup melted butter, 1/4 cup erythritol.

For the filling: 3/4 cup almond milk, zest and juice of 2 lemons, 1/4 cup erythritol, 2 egg yolks, 1 tsp agar-agar (as thickener).

M.C.: Baking and chilling

Procedure:

Combine crust ingredients; press into tart pan; bake at 350°F for 10 minutes.

Heat almond milk, lemon zest, juice, erythritol, egg yolks, and agar-agar until thickened; pour into crust.

Chill until set; garnish with lemon slices.

N.V.: Calories: 200, Fat: 18g, Carbs: 6g (net), Protein: 6g.

Recipe 3: Rustic Apple Cinnamon Tart

P.T.: 40 minutes + chilling

Ingr:

For the crust: 1 1/2 cups almond flour, 1/4 cup coconut flour, 1/4 cup butter (cold, cubed), 1 egg.

For the filling: 2 medium apples (thinly

sliced), 1 tsp cinnamon, 1/4 cup erythritol, 1 tbsp lemon juice.

M.C.: Baking

Procedure:

Pulse crust ingredients in a food processor; press into tart pan; chill.

Toss apple slices with cinnamon, erythritol, and lemon juice; arrange on crust.

Bake at 375°F for 25 minutes; cool before serving.

N.V.: Calories: 190, Fat: 15g, Carbs: 10g (net), Protein: 4g.

Recipe 4: No-Bake Coconut Mango Tart

P.T.: 25 minutes + chilling

Ingr:

For the crust: 1 cup unsweetened shredded coconut, 1/2 cup almond flour, 1/4 cup coconut oil, 2 tbsp erythritol.

For the filling: 1 large mango (pureed), 1/4 cup coconut cream, 2 tbsp erythritol, 1 tsp lime zest, 1 tbsp gelatin (dissolved in water).

M.C.: No-bake

Procedure:

Mix crust ingredients; press into a tart pan; chill.

Combine mango puree, coconut cream, erythritol, lime zest, and gelatin; pour over crust.

Chill until set; garnish with mango slices and lime zest.

N.V.: Calories: 220, Fat: 18g, Carbs: 12g (net), Protein: 3g.

Recipe 5: Chocolate Raspberry Dream Tart

P.T.: 30 minutes + chilling

Ingr:

For the crust: 2 cups almond flour, 1/4 cup cocoa powder, 1/4 cup melted butter, 3 tbsp erythritol.

For the filling: 1 cup fresh raspberries, 1/2 cup sugar-free dark chocolate (melted), 1/4 cup heavy cream, 1/4 cup erythritol.

M.C.: No-bake

Procedure:

Mix crust ingredients; press into tart pan; chill.

Blend raspberries, melted chocolate, heavy cream, and erythritol; pour over crust.

Chill until set; garnish with fresh raspberries.

N.V.: Calories: 250, Fat: 22g, Carbs: 8g (net), Protein: 6g.

Recipe 6: Key Lime Avocado Tart

P.T.: 30 minutes + chilling

Ingr:

For the crust: 1 1/2 cups almond flour, 1/4 cup coconut oil, 2 tbsp erythritol.

For the filling: 2 ripe avocados, juice and zest of 4 key limes, 1/4 cup erythritol, 1/4 cup coconut cream, 1 tsp vanilla extract.

M.C.: No-bake

Procedure:

Combine crust ingredients; press into tart pan; chill.

Blend filling ingredients until smooth; pour into crust.

Chill until firm; garnish with lime slices and zest.

N.V.: Calories: 230, Fat: 20g, Carbs: 9g (net), Protein: 4g.

Recipe 7: Strawberry Basil Balsamic Tart

P.T.: 35 minutes + chilling

Ingr:

For the crust: 1 cup almond flour, 1/2 cup walnut flour, 1/4 cup melted butter, 2 tbsp erythritol.

For the filling: 1 cup strawberries (sliced), 1/4 cup sugar-free balsamic reduction, 1 tbsp

chopped fresh basil, 1/4 cup erythritol, 1 cup whipped cream (sugar-free).

M.C.: No-bake

Procedure:

Mix crust ingredients; press into tart pan; chill.

Arrange strawberry slices over crust; sprinkle with erythritol and basil.

Drizzle with balsamic reduction; top with whipped cream.

Chill until ready to serve.

N.V.: Calories: 210, Fat: 18g, Carbs: 8g (net), Protein: 5g.

Classic Pies with a Diabetic-Friendly Twist

Recipe 1: Keto Apple Pie

P.T.: 1 hour

Ingr:

For the crust: 2 cups almond flour, 1/3 cup coconut oil (solid), 1 egg, pinch of salt.

For the filling: 3 cups zucchini (peeled,

diced, and cooked to resemble apples), 1 tbsp lemon juice, 1/3 cup erythritol, 2 tsp cinnamon, 1/4 tsp nutmeg.

M.C.: Baking

Procedure:

Prepare the crust by mixing ingredients, then press into a pie dish and pre-bake at 350°F for 10 minutes.

Mix the "apple" filling ingredients, simmer until tender.

Fill the crust with the zucchini mixture, cover with lattice top, bake for 45 minutes.

N.V.: Calories: 250, Fat: 22g, Carbs: 8g (net), Protein: 6g.

Recipe 2: Sugar-Free Pumpkin Pie

P.T.: 50 minutes

Ingr:

For the crust: 1 1/2 cups almond flour, 1/4 cup unsalted butter, melted, 1 egg.

For the filling: 1 can (15 oz) pumpkin puree, 3/4 cup heavy cream, 1/2 cup erythritol, 2 eggs, 1 tsp vanilla extract, 2 tsp pumpkin pie spice.

M.C.: Baking

Procedure:

Mix crust ingredients, press into pie dish, and bake at 350°F for 8 minutes.

Whisk together filling ingredients, pour into pre-baked crust.

Bake for 40 minutes, or until set.

N.V.: Calories: 210, Fat: 19g, Carbs: 6g (net), Protein: 5g.

Recipe 3: Low-Carb Pecan Pie

P.T.: 1 hour

Ingr:

For the crust: 2 cups almond flour, 1/4 cup butter (melted), 2 tbsp erythritol.

For the filling: 1 cup pecans (halved), 3 eggs, 1 cup sugar-free maple syrup, 2 tbsp butter (melted), 1 tsp vanilla extract.

M.C.: Baking

Procedure:

Prepare the crust and pre-bake at 350°F for 10 minutes.

Arrange pecans in the crust.

Mix remaining ingredients and pour over pecans.

Bake for 50 minutes or until filling is set.

N.V.: Calories: 320, Fat: 30g, Carbs: 5g (net), Protein: 6g.

Recipe 4: Lemon Meringue Pie (Low-Carb)

P.T.: 1 hour 15 minutes

Ingr:

For the crust: 2 cups almond flour, 1/4 cup butter (melted), 1 egg.

For the filling: 1/2 cup lemon juice, zest of 1 lemon, 1/2 cup erythritol, 2 eggs + 2 egg yolks, 1/4 cup butter.

For the meringue: 4 egg whites, 1/4 tsp cream of tartar, 1/4 cup erythritol.

M.C.: Baking

Procedure:

Form crust and pre-bake.

Cook filling ingredients until thickened, fill crust.

Whip meringue ingredients, top pie, bake until golden.

N.V.: Calories: 270, Fat: 23g, Carbs: 7g

(net), Protein: 8g.

Recipe 5: Raspberry Almond Tart

P.T.: 30 minutes + chilling

Ingr:

For the crust: 2 cups almond flour, 1/3 cup melted coconut oil, 2 tbsp erythritol.

For the filling: 2 cups fresh raspberries, 1/4 cup sugar-free raspberry jam, 1/4 cup sliced almonds.

M.C.: No-bake

Procedure:

Mix crust ingredients, press into tart pan, chill.

Spread jam over crust, top with raspberries and almonds.

Chill until set.

N.V.: Calories: 220, Fat: 18g, Carbs: 10g (net), Protein: 6g.

Recipe 6: Chocolate Silk Pie

P.T.: 45 minutes + chilling

Ingr:

For the crust: 1 3/4 cups almond flour, 1/4 cup cocoa powder, 1/4 cup melted butter, 1 egg.

For the filling: 1 1/2 cups heavy cream, 1 cup sugar-free dark chocolate chips, 1/2 cup erythritol, 2 tsp vanilla extract.

M.C.: Baking and chilling

Procedure:

Bake the crust at 350°F for 10 minutes. Cool.

Melt chocolate, mix with other filling ingredients, pour into crust.

Chill until firm.

N.V.: Calories: 330, Fat: 29g, Carbs: 9g (net), Protein: 7g.

Recipe 7: Key Lime Pie

P.T.: 30 minutes + chilling

Ingr:

For the crust: 1 1/2 cups almond flour, 1/4 cup butter (melted), 2 tbsp erythritol.

For the filling: 1 cup heavy cream, 1/2 cup key lime juice, zest of 3 key limes, 1/2 cup erythritol, 2 egg yolks.

M.C.: Baking and chilling

Procedure:

Mix crust ingredients, press into pie dish, bake at 350°F for 10 minutes.

Whisk filling ingredients, pour into crust, bake for 15 minutes.

Chill for at least 2 hours.

N.V.: Calories: 310, Fat: 28g, Carbs: 8g (net), Protein: 5g.

Chapter 6: Muffins & Breads for Breakfast or Tea Time

High-Fiber Muffins for a Healthy Start

Recipe 1: Chia & Blueberry Muffins

P.T.: 35 minutes

Ingr:

1 1/2 cups almond flour

1/4 cup coconut flour

1/4 cup chia seeds

1/2 cup erythritol

1 tsp baking powder

1/2 tsp baking soda

1/4 tsp salt

3 large eggs

1/3 cup unsweetened almond milk

1/4 cup coconut oil, melted

1 tsp vanilla extract

1 cup fresh or frozen blueberries

M.C.: Baking

Procedure:

Preheat oven to 350°F (175°C) and line a muffin tin with paper liners.

In a large bowl, mix together almond flour, coconut flour, chia seeds, erythritol, baking powder, baking soda, and salt.

In another bowl, whisk together eggs, almond milk, melted coconut oil, and vanilla extract.

Combine wet and dry ingredients, gently fold in blueberries.

Divide batter among muffin cups and bake for 20-25 minutes or until a toothpick inserted into the center comes out clean.

N.V.: Estimated per muffin: Calories: 180, Fat: 14g, Carbs: 10g (net), Fiber: 4g, Protein: 6g.

Recipe 2: Flaxseed & Walnut Breakfast Muffins

P.T.: 40 minutes

Ingr:

1 cup flaxseed meal

1/2 cup almond flour

1/4 cup walnuts, chopped

1/4 cup erythritol

1 tsp cinnamon

1 tsp baking powder

1/2 tsp salt

4 eggs

1/4 cup unsweetened almond milk

1/4 cup olive oil

1 tsp apple cider vinegar

M.C.: Baking

Procedure:

Preheat oven to 350°F (175°C) and prepare a muffin tin with liners.

Combine flaxseed meal, almond flour, chopped walnuts, erythritol, cinnamon, baking powder, and salt in a bowl.

In another bowl, beat eggs, then mix in almond milk, olive oil, and apple cider vinegar.

Merge the wet ingredients with the dry, stirring until just combined.

Spoon batter into muffin cups, bake for 22-25 minutes, or until a toothpick comes out clean.

N.V.: Estimated per muffin: Calories: 160, Fat: 12g, Carbs: 5g (net), Fiber: 3g, Protein: 5g.

Recipe 3: Apple Cinnamon Fiber Muffins

P.T.: 30 minutes

Ingr:

1 1/2 cups almond flour

1/2 cup oat fiber (ensure gluten-free if necessary)

1/4 cup erythritol

2 tsp cinnamon

1 tsp baking powder

1/2 tsp baking soda

1/4 tsp salt

2 eggs

1/2 cup unsweetened applesauce

1/4 cup coconut oil, melted

1 tsp vanilla extract

1 medium apple, peeled and diced

M.C.: Baking

Procedure:

Preheat the oven to 350°F (175°C), line a muffin pan with paper liners.

Mix almond flour, oat fiber, erythritol, cinnamon, baking powder, baking soda, and salt in a large bowl.

In a separate bowl, whisk eggs, applesauce, melted coconut oil, and vanilla.

Stir wet ingredients into dry until combined, fold in diced apple.

Distribute batter into muffin cups, bake for 18-20 minutes.

N.V.: Estimated per muffin: Calories: 150, Fat: 11g, Carbs: 8g (net), Fiber: 5g, Protein: 4g.

Recipe 4: Pumpkin Seed & Avocado Oil Muffins

P.T.: 35 minutes

Ingr:

1 cup almond flour

1/2 cup pumpkin seeds, ground into meal

1/4 cup erythritol

1 tsp pumpkin pie spice

1 tsp baking powder

1/2 tsp salt

3 eggs

1/4 cup avocado oil

1/4 cup unsweetened almond milk

1/2 cup pumpkin puree

M.C.: Baking

Procedure:

Preheat oven to 350°F (175°C) and line a muffin tin.

Combine almond flour, ground pumpkin seeds, erythritol, pumpkin pie spice, baking powder, and salt.

Whisk together eggs, avocado oil, almond milk, and pumpkin puree.

Mix wet ingredients into dry until well combined.

Fill muffin cups and bake for 23-25 minutes.

N.V.: Estimated per muffin: Calories: 170, Fat: 14g, Carbs: 6g (net), Fiber: 3g, Protein: 5g.

Recipe 5: Carrot & Ginger Fiber Muffins

P.T.: 30 minutes

Ingr:

1 cup almond flour

1/2 cup coconut flour

1/4 cup erythritol

2 tsp ginger, grated

1 tsp cinnamon

1 tsp baking powder

1/2 tsp salt

3 eggs

1/4 cup coconut oil, melted

1/2 cup unsweetened almond milk

1 cup carrots, grated

M.C.: Baking

Procedure:

Preheat oven to 350°F (175°C), prepare muffin tin with liners.

Mix almond and coconut flours, erythritol, ginger, cinnamon, baking powder, and salt.

Combine eggs, coconut oil, almond milk, then add to dry ingredients.

Fold in grated carrots.

Spoon into muffin cups, bake for 20 minutes.

N.V.: Estimated per muffin: Calories: 140, Fat: 10g, Carbs: 7g (net), Fiber: 4g, Protein: 4g.

Recipe 6: Spicy Zucchini Oat Muffins

P.T.: 40 minutes

Ingr:

1 cup almond flour

1/2 cup rolled oats (gluten-free if necessary)

1/4 cup flaxseed meal

1/4 cup erythritol

1 tsp cinnamon

1/2 tsp nutmeg

1 tsp baking powder

1/2 tsp baking soda

1/4 tsp salt

2 eggs

1/4 cup olive oil

1/2 cup unsweetened almond milk

1 cup zucchini, grated and excess moisture squeezed out

M.C.: Baking

Procedure:

Preheat oven to 350°F (175°C), line muffin tin.

Mix dry ingredients except erythritol in a bowl.

In another bowl, beat eggs with erythritol, stir in olive oil and almond milk.

Combine wet and dry ingredients, fold in zucchini.

Fill muffin cups, bake for 25 minutes.

N.V.: Estimated per muffin: Calories: 160, Fat: 12g, Carbs: 9g (net), Fiber: 3g, Protein: 5g.

Recipe 7: Cocoa & Beet Fiber Muffins

P.T.: 35 minutes

Ingr:

1 cup almond flour

1/2 cup cocoa powder (unsweetened)

1/4 cup ground flaxseed

1/4 cup erythritol

1 tsp baking powder

1/2 tsp salt

3 eggs

1/4 cup unsweetened almond milk

1/4 cup coconut oil, melted

1 cup beets, cooked and pureed

M.C.: Baking

Procedure:

Preheat oven to 350°F (175°C), line muffin pan.

Combine dry ingredients in a large bowl.

Mix eggs, almond milk, coconut oil, and beet puree in another bowl.

Stir wet ingredients into dry, mix until combined.

Distribute batter into muffin cups, bake for 20-22 minutes.

N.V.: Estimated per muffin: Calories: 150, Fat: 11g, Carbs: 8g (net), Fiber: 4g, Protein: 5g.

Sweet and Savory Quick Breads

Recipe 1: Zucchini Cheddar Bread

P.T.: 60 minutes

Ingr:

2 cups almond flour

1/2 cup grated sharp cheddar cheese

1 cup grated zucchini (water squeezed out)

3 eggs

1/4 cup olive oil

1 tsp baking powder

1/2 tsp salt

1/4 tsp garlic powder

M.C.: Baking

Procedure:

Preheat the oven to 350°F (175°C). Grease a loaf pan.

Mix almond flour, baking powder, salt, and garlic powder in a bowl.

In another bowl, whisk eggs and olive oil. Stir in grated zucchini and cheddar.

Combine wet and dry ingredients until just mixed. Pour into prepared pan.

Bake for 45-50 minutes or until a toothpick inserted comes out clean.

N.V.: Estimated per serving: Calories: 220, Fat: 18g, Carbs: 5g (net), Protein: 9g.

Recipe 2: Lemon Poppy Seed Loaf

P.T.: 50 minutes

Ingr:

2 cups almond flour

1/3 cup erythritol

1/4 cup poppy seeds

3 eggs

1/4 cup unsweetened almond milk

1/4 cup coconut oil, melted

Zest and juice of 1 lemon

1 tsp baking powder

M.C.: Baking

Procedure:

Preheat oven to 350°F (175°C) and line a loaf pan with parchment paper.

Combine almond flour, erythritol, poppy seeds, and baking powder in a large bowl.

In a separate bowl, mix eggs, almond milk, melted coconut oil, lemon zest, and lemon juice.

Fold wet ingredients into dry ingredients until well combined.

Pour batter into prepared loaf pan and bake for 40-45 minutes.

N.V.: Estimated per serving: Calories: 210, Fat: 17g, Carbs: 6g (net), Protein: 7g.

Recipe 3: Cranberry Walnut Bread

P.T.: 55 minutes

Ingr:

2 cups almond flour

1/2 cup erythritol

1 cup fresh or frozen cranberries

1/2 cup walnuts, chopped

3 eggs

1/4 cup unsweetened almond milk

1/4 cup olive oil

1 tsp vanilla extract

1 tsp baking powder

M.C.: Baking

Procedure:

Preheat oven to 350°F (175°C). Grease and flour a loaf pan.

Mix almond flour, erythritol, and baking powder in a large bowl.

Beat eggs, almond milk, olive oil, and vanilla in another bowl.

Combine wet ingredients with dry, fold in cranberries and walnuts.

Pour into loaf pan, bake for 45 minutes, or until golden.

N.V.: Estimated per serving: Calories: 230, Fat: 19g, Carbs: 7g (net), Protein: 8g.

Recipe 4: Savory Olive and Herb Bread

P.T.: 50 minutes

Ingr:

2 cups almond flour

1/4 cup coconut flour

1/2 cup kalamata olives, pitted and chopped

2 tbsp fresh rosemary, chopped

3 eggs

1/4 cup olive oil

1/2 cup water

1 tsp baking powder

1/2 tsp salt

M.C.: Baking

Procedure:

Preheat oven to 350°F (175°C) and line a loaf pan with parchment.

Combine almond flour, coconut flour, baking powder, and salt.

Stir in eggs, olive oil, and water until smooth. Fold in olives and rosemary.

Transfer to loaf pan, bake for 40 minutes, or until a toothpick comes out clean.

N.V.: Estimated per serving: Calories: 210, Fat: 18g, Carbs: 6g (net), Protein: 7g.

Recipe 5: Cinnamon Swirl Breakfast Bread

P.T.: 60 minutes

Ingr:

2 cups almond flour

1/4 cup erythritol, plus 2 tbsp for the swirl

3 eggs

1/4 cup unsweetened almond milk

1/4 cup butter, melted

1 tbsp cinnamon for the swirl

1 tsp baking powder

M.C.: Baking

Procedure:

Preheat oven to 350°F (175°C). Prepare a loaf pan.

Mix almond flour, 1/4 cup erythritol, and baking powder. Add eggs, almond milk, and melted butter.

Pour half the batter into the pan. Mix 2 tbsp erythritol with cinnamon, sprinkle over batter.

Top with remaining batter, use a knife to

swirl. Bake for 50 minutes.

N.V.: Estimated per serving: Calories: 220, Fat: 20g, Carbs: 5g (net), Protein: 8g.

Recipe 6: Blueberry Lemon Loaf

P.T.: 55 minutes

Ingr:

2 cups almond flour

1/2 cup erythritol

1 cup blueberries (fresh or frozen)

Zest of 1 lemon

3 eggs

1/4 cup unsweetened almond milk

1/4 cup coconut oil, melted

1 tsp vanilla extract

1 tsp baking powder

M.C.: Baking

Procedure:

Preheat oven to 350°F (175°C). Line a loaf pan with parchment.

Whisk together almond flour, erythritol, and baking powder. Add eggs, almond milk, melted coconut oil, lemon zest, and vanilla.

Gently fold in blueberries. Pour into prepared pan.

Bake for 45-50 minutes or until a toothpick inserted comes out clean.

N.V.: Estimated per serving: Calories: 220, Fat: 18g, Carbs: 8g (net), Fiber: 3g, Protein: 6g.

Recipe 7: Choco-Almond Banana Bread

P.T.: 1 hour

Ingr:

2 cups almond flour

1/4 cup cocoa powder

1/2 cup erythritol

3 ripe bananas, mashed

3 eggs

1/4 cup unsweetened almond milk

1/4 cup olive oil

1 tsp vanilla extract

1 tsp baking powder

1/2 cup sugar-free dark chocolate chips

M.C.: Baking

Procedure:

Preheat oven to 350°F (175°C). Grease and flour a loaf pan.

Mix almond flour, cocoa powder, erythritol, and baking powder.

Blend bananas, eggs, almond milk, olive oil, and vanilla. Combine with dry ingredients.

Fold in chocolate chips, pour into pan, and

bake for 55 minutes.

N.V.: Estimated per serving: Calories: 230, Fat: 17g, Carbs: 10g (net), Fiber: 4g, Protein: 7g.

Tea Time Treats: Scones and Biscotti

Recipe 1: Almond Flour Lemon Scones

P.T.: 25 minutes

Ingr:

2 cups almond flour

1/3 cup erythritol

Zest of 1 lemon

1 tsp baking powder

1/4 tsp salt

2 large eggs

1/4 cup unsweetened almond milk

1 tsp vanilla extract

M.C.: Baking

Procedure:

Preheat oven to 350°F (175°C) and line a baking sheet with parchment paper.

In a large bowl, combine almond flour, erythritol, lemon zest, baking powder, and salt.

In a separate bowl, whisk together eggs, almond milk, and vanilla extract.

Mix wet ingredients into dry until dough forms.

Form dough into a circle on the prepared baking sheet, then cut into wedges.

Bake for 18-20 minutes or until golden.

N.V.: Estimated per serving: Calories: 180, Fat: 15g, Carbs: 6g (net), Protein: 7g.

Recipe 2: Cranberry Orange Biscotti

P.T.: 50 minutes

Ingr:

2 cups almond flour

1/2 cup erythritol

1/2 cup dried cranberries, chopped

Zest of 1 orange

2 eggs

1 tsp vanilla extract

1/2 tsp baking powder

M.C.: Baking

Procedure:

Preheat oven to 325°F (163°C) and line a baking sheet with parchment paper.

Combine almond flour, erythritol, cranberries, orange zest, and baking powder in a bowl.

Beat in eggs and vanilla until a dough forms.

Form a log with the dough, bake for 25 minutes, then slice and bake again until crisp.

N.V.: Estimated per serving: Calories: 160, Fat: 12g, Carbs: 8g (net), Protein: 6g.

Recipe 3: Coconut Chia Seed Scones

P.T.: 30 minutes

Ingr:

1 3/4 cups almond flour

1/4 cup coconut flour

1/4 cup chia seeds

1/3 cup erythritol

1 tsp baking powder

1/4 cup unsweetened shredded coconut

1/4 cup coconut oil, melted

2 eggs

1 tsp vanilla extract

M.C.: Baking

Procedure:

Preheat oven to 350°F (175°C).

Mix all dry ingredients in a bowl. Stir in melted coconut oil, eggs, and vanilla until dough forms.

Shape into a round disc on a baking sheet, cut into wedges, and separate slightly.

Bake for 20-22 minutes or until edges are golden.

N.V.: Estimated per serving: Calories: 190, Fat: 15g, Carbs: 7g (net), Protein: 5g.

Recipe 4: Espresso Chocolate Biscotti

P.T.: 55 minutes

Ingr:

2 cups almond flour

1/4 cup unsweetened cocoa powder

1/2 cup erythritol

1 tbsp instant espresso powder

2 eggs

1 tsp vanilla extract

1/2 tsp baking powder

1/4 cup sugar-free dark chocolate chips

M.C.: Baking

Procedure:

Preheat oven to 325°F (163°C).

Mix almond flour, cocoa powder, erythritol, espresso powder, and baking powder.

Whisk in eggs and vanilla, fold in chocolate chips.

Form a log on a baking sheet, slice after initial bake, then bake slices until crisp.

N.V.: Estimated per serving: Calories: 170, Fat: 14g, Carbs: 6g (net), Protein: 7g.

Recipe 5: Lemon Lavender Scones

P.T.: 30 minutes

Ingr:

2 cups almond flour

1/3 cup erythritol

2 tsp dried lavender flowers

Zest of 1 lemon

1 tsp baking powder

1/4 tsp salt

2 eggs

1/4 cup unsweetened almond milk

1/2 tsp vanilla extract

M.C.: Baking

Procedure:

Preheat the oven to 350°F (175°C).

Combine almond flour, erythritol, lavender, lemon zest, baking powder, and salt.

Beat in eggs, almond milk, and vanilla. Form into a circle, cut into wedges, and bake.

N.V.: Estimated per serving: Calories: 180, Fat: 15g, Carbs: 7g (net), Protein: 6g.

Recipe 6: Pistachio Rosewater Biscotti

P.T.: 1 hour

Ingr:

2 cups almond flour

1/2 cup erythritol

1/2 cup pistachios, chopped

1 tsp rosewater

2 eggs

1/2 tsp baking powder

M.C.: Baking

Procedure:

Preheat oven to 325°F (163°C).

Mix almond flour, erythritol, pistachios, and baking powder. Stir in eggs and rosewater until dough forms.

Form a log, bake, slice, and bake slices again until dry.

N.V.: Estimated per serving: Calories: 160, Fat: 13g, Carbs: 7g (net), Protein: 6g.

Recipe 7: Cheddar and Chive Scones

P.T.: 35 minutes

Ingr:

2 cups almond flour

1/4 cup coconut flour

1/3 cup grated sharp cheddar cheese

1/4 cup fresh chives, chopped

2 eggs

1/4 cup heavy cream

1 tsp baking powder

1/2 tsp garlic powder

1/4 tsp salt

M.C.: Baking

Procedure:

Preheat oven to 350°F (175°C).

Combine all ingredients in a bowl until a dough forms.

Shape into a round disc, cut into wedges, bake until golden and firm.

N.V.: Estimated per serving: Calories: 220, Fat: 18g, Carbs: 6g (net), Protein: 9g.

Chapter 7: Frozen Treats to Beat the Heat

Sugar-Free Ice Creams and Sorbets

Recipe 1: Creamy Avocado Lime Ice Cream

P.T.: 4 hours (including freezing time)

Ingr:

2 ripe avocados

Juice and zest of 2 limes

1/3 cup erythritol

1 can (14 oz) full-fat coconut milk

1 tsp vanilla extract

M.C.: Blending and Freezing

Procedure:

Blend avocados, lime juice, lime zest, erythritol, coconut milk, and vanilla extract until smooth.

Pour mixture into an ice cream maker and churn according to the manufacturer's instructions.

Transfer to a freezer-safe container and freeze until firm, about 3-4 hours.

N.V.: Estimated per serving: Calories: 200, Fat: 18g, Carbs: 8g (net), Protein: 2g.

Recipe 2: Berry Blast Sorbet

P.T.: 3 hours (including freezing time)

Ingr:

2 cups mixed berries (strawberries, blueberries, raspberries)

1/4 cup erythritol

1/2 cup water

Juice of 1 lemon

M.C.: Blending and Freezing

Procedure:

Blend berries, erythritol, water, and lemon juice until smooth.

Pour through a sieve to remove seeds, if desired.

Freeze in an ice cream maker or pour into a container and stir every 30 minutes until frozen.

N.V.: Estimated per serving: Calories: 50, Fat: 0g, Carbs: 12g (net), Protein: 1g.

Recipe 3: Chocolate Peanut Butter Keto Ice Cream

P.T.: 4 hours (including freezing time)

Ingr:

1 can (14 oz) full-fat coconut milk

1/4 cup unsweetened cocoa powder

1/3 cup natural peanut butter

1/4 cup erythritol

1 tsp vanilla extract

M.C.: Blending and Freezing

Procedure:

Blend coconut milk, cocoa powder, peanut butter, erythritol, and vanilla until smooth.

Churn in an ice cream maker or freeze, stirring occasionally, until set.

N.V.: Estimated per serving: Calories: 220, Fat: 20g, Carbs: 6g (net), Protein: 5g.

Recipe 4: Mint Chocolate Chip Ice Cream

P.T.: 4 hours (including freezing time)

Ingr:

1 can (14 oz) full-fat coconut milk

1/3 cup erythritol

1/2 tsp mint extract (adjust to taste)

1/4 cup sugar-free dark chocolate chips

M.C.: Blending and Freezing

Procedure:

Blend coconut milk, erythritol, and mint extract until smooth.

Churn in an ice cream maker, adding chocolate chips in the last few minutes. Freeze until firm.

N.V.: Estimated per serving: Calories: 210, Fat: 19g, Carbs: 7g (net), Protein: 2g.

Recipe 5: Cinnamon Toast Ice Cream

P.T.: 4 hours (including freezing time)

Ingr:

1 can (14 oz) full-fat coconut milk

1/4 cup erythritol

1 tsp cinnamon

1 tsp vanilla extract

M.C.: Blending and Freezing

Procedure:

Blend coconut milk, erythritol, cinnamon, and vanilla until smooth.

Churn in an ice cream maker or freeze, stirring occasionally, until set.

N.V.: Estimated per serving: Calories: 200, Fat: 18g, Carbs: 5g (net), Protein: 1g.

Recipe 6: Tropical Mango Sorbet

P.T.: 3 hours (including freezing time)

Ingr:

2 cups fresh mango, chopped

1/4 cup erythritol

Juice of 1 lime

M.C.: Blending and Freezing

Procedure:

Blend mango, erythritol, and lime juice until smooth.

Freeze in an ice cream maker or in a container, stirring occasionally, until set.

N.V.: Estimated per serving: Calories: 60, Fat: 0g, Carbs: 15g (net), Protein: 1g.

Recipe 7: Raspberry Lemonade

Ice Cream

P.T.: 4 hours (including freezing time)

Ingr:

1 can (14 oz) full-fat coconut milk

1 cup fresh raspberries

1/4 cup erythritol

Juice and zest of 2 lemons

M.C.: Blending and Freezing

Procedure:

Blend coconut milk, raspberries, erythritol, lemon juice, and zest until smooth.

Strain to remove raspberry seeds, then churn in an ice cream maker or freeze, stirring occasionally.

N.V.: Estimated per serving: Calories: 150, Fat: 12g, Carbs: 8g (net), Protein: 2g.

Frozen Yogurt and Popsicles

Recipe 1: Greek Yogurt Berry Popsicles

P.T.: 4 hours (including freezing time)

Ingr:

2 cups Greek yogurt, unsweetened

1/2 cup mixed berries (strawberries, blueberries, raspberries), pureed

1/4 cup erythritol or stevia to taste

1 tsp vanilla extract

M.C.: Freezing

Procedure:

Mix Greek yogurt with erythritol and vanilla extract until well combined.

Fold in the pureed berries, creating a marbled effect.

Pour the mixture into popsicle molds, insert sticks, and freeze until solid.

N.V.: Estimated per serving: Calories: 80, Fat: 0.5g, Carbs: 6g (net), Protein: 12g.

Recipe 2: Keto Chocolate Fudge Pops

P.T.: 5 hours (including freezing time)

Ingr:

1 can (13.5 oz) coconut milk, full-fat

1/4 cup unsweetened cocoa powder

1/4 cup erythritol

1/2 tsp vanilla extract

Pinch of salt

M.C.: Freezing

Procedure:

Blend all ingredients until smooth.

Pour the mixture into popsicle molds and freeze for at least 5 hours, until firm.

N.V.: Estimated per serving: Calories: 150, Fat: 14g, Carbs: 4g (net), Protein: 2g.

Recipe 3: Lemon Cucumber Mint Yogurt Pops

P.T.: 4 hours (including freezing time)

Ingr:

2 cups Greek yogurt, unsweetened

Juice and zest of 1 lemon

1/2 cup cucumber, finely diced

1/4 cup fresh mint leaves, minced

1/4 cup erythritol

M.C.: Freezing

Procedure:

Mix all ingredients in a bowl until thoroughly combined.

Pour into popsicle molds and freeze until solid.

N.V.: Estimated per serving: Calories: 75, Fat: 0.5g, Carbs: 5g (net), Protein: 11g.

Recipe 4: Avocado Lime Frozen Yogurt

P.T.: 4 hours (including freezing time)

Ingr:

2 ripe avocados

2 cups Greek yogurt, unsweetened

Juice and zest of 2 limes

1/3 cup erythritol

1 tsp vanilla extract

M.C.: Blending and Freezing

Procedure:

Blend all ingredients until creamy.

Pour into a freezer-safe container and freeze, stirring every hour, until desired consistency is reached.

N.V.: Estimated per serving: Calories: 200, Fat: 15g, Carbs: 8g (net), Protein: 10g.

Recipe 5: Strawberry Basil Popsicles

P.T.: 4 hours (including freezing time)

Ingr:

2 cups strawberries, hulled

1/4 cup erythritol

1/4 cup water

10 basil leaves

M.C.: Blending and Freezing

Procedure:

Puree strawberries, erythritol, water, and basil leaves until smooth.

Pour into popsicle molds and freeze until solid.

N.V.: Estimated per serving: Calories: 30, Fat: 0g, Carbs: 7g (net), Protein: 0g.

Recipe 6: Coconut Almond Swirl Frozen Yogurt

P.T.: 5 hours (including freezing time)

Ingr:

2 cups Greek yogurt, unsweetened

1/4 cup almond butter

1/4 cup coconut milk

1/4 cup erythritol

1 tsp almond extract

M.C.: Freezing

Procedure:

Mix Greek yogurt with erythritol and almond extract.

Swirl in almond butter and coconut milk.

Freeze in a container, stirring occasionally, until set.

N.V.: Estimated per serving: Calories: 180, Fat: 14g, Carbs: 5g (net), Protein: 10g.

Recipe 7: Peach Ginger Yogurt Pops

P.T.: 4 hours (including freezing time)

Ingr:

2 cups Greek yogurt, unsweetened

1 cup peaches, diced

1/4 cup erythritol

1 tbsp fresh ginger, grated

M.C.: Freezing

Procedure:

Blend peaches, erythritol, and ginger until smooth.

Fold mixture into Greek yogurt, pour into popsicle molds.

Freeze until solid.

N.V.: Estimated per serving: Calories: 90, Fat: 0.5g, Carbs: 8g (net), Protein: 12g.

Diabetic-Friendly Ice Cream Cake

Recipe 1: Vanilla Berry Layer Ice Cream Cake

P.T.: 6 hours (including freezing time)

Ingr:

For Vanilla Ice Cream Layer:

2 cups heavy cream

1 cup unsweetened almond milk

1/3 cup erythritol

2 tsp vanilla extract

For Berry Sorbet Layer:

2 cups mixed berries (fresh or frozen)

1/4 cup erythritol

1/4 cup water

Juice of 1 lemon

For the Crust:

1 1/2 cups almond flour

1/4 cup coconut oil, melted

2 tbsp erythritol

M.C.: Freezing

Procedure:

Crust: Mix almond flour, coconut oil, and erythritol. Press into the bottom of a springform pan. Freeze for 30 minutes.

Vanilla Ice Cream: Whip heavy cream, almond milk, erythritol, and vanilla. Pour over the crust and freeze for 2 hours.

Berry Sorbet: Blend berries, erythritol, water, and lemon juice. Pour over frozen vanilla layer. Freeze for at least 3 hours.

N.V.: Estimated per serving: Calories: 250, Fat: 22g, Carbs: 6g (net), Protein: 3g.

set.

N.V.: Estimated per serving: Calories: 300, Fat: 25g, Carbs: 7g (net), Protein: 8g.

Recipe 2: Keto Chocolate Peanut Butter Ice Cream Cake

P.T.: 5 hours (including freezing time)

Ingr:

For Chocolate Ice Cream Layer:

2 cups heavy cream

1 cup unsweetened almond milk

1/3 cup erythritol

1/4 cup unsweetened cocoa powder

For Peanut Butter Layer:

1 cup natural peanut butter (unsweetened)

1/4 cup erythritol

1/4 cup heavy cream

For the Crust:

1 1/2 cups crushed pecans

1/4 cup butter, melted

2 tbsp erythritol

M.C.: Freezing

Procedure:

Crust: Combine crushed pecans, melted butter, and erythritol. Press into the bottom of a springform pan. Freeze for 20 minutes.

Chocolate Ice Cream: Mix heavy cream, almond milk, erythritol, and cocoa powder. Pour over crust and freeze for 2 hours.

Peanut Butter Layer: Mix peanut butter, erythritol, and heavy cream until smooth. Spread over the chocolate layer. Freeze until

Recipe 3: Mint Chocolate Chip Ice Cream Cake

P.T.: 6 hours (including freezing time)

Ingr:

For Mint Ice Cream Layer:

2 cups heavy cream

1 cup unsweetened almond milk

1/3 cup erythritol

1/2 tsp mint extract

1/4 cup sugar-free dark chocolate chips

For the Crust:

1 1/2 cups almond flour

1/4 cup cocoa powder

1/4 cup coconut oil, melted

2 tbsp erythritol

M.C.: Freezing

Procedure:

Crust: Mix almond flour, cocoa powder, coconut oil, and erythritol. Press into a springform pan. Freeze for 30 minutes.

Mint Ice Cream: Whip heavy cream, almond milk, erythritol, and mint extract. Fold in chocolate chips. Pour over crust and freeze until set.

N.V.: Estimated per serving: Calories: 270, Fat: 24g, Carbs: 5g (net), Protein: 4g.

Recipe 4: Strawberry Cheesecake Ice Cream Cake

P.T.: 6 hours (including freezing time)

Ingr:

For Strawberry Ice Cream Layer:

2 cups heavy cream

1 cup unsweetened almond milk

1/3 cup erythritol

1 cup strawberries, pureed

For Cheesecake Layer:

1 cup cream cheese, softened

1/4 cup erythritol

1 tsp vanilla extract

For the Crust:

1 1/2 cups almond flour

1/4 cup butter, melted

2 tbsp erythritol

M.C.: Freezing

Procedure:

Crust: Combine almond flour, melted butter, and erythritol. Press into a springform pan. Freeze for 20 minutes.

Strawberry Ice Cream: Blend heavy cream, almond milk, erythritol, and strawberry puree. Pour over crust and freeze for 2 hours.

Cheesecake Layer: Mix cream cheese, erythritol, and vanilla. Spread over strawberry layer. Freeze until firm.

N.V.: Estimated per serving: Calories: 280, Fat: 26g, Carbs: 6g (net), Protein: 5g.

Recipe 5: Lemon Blueberry Ice Cream Cake

P.T.: 5 hours (including freezing time)

Ingr:

For Lemon Ice Cream Layer:

2 cups heavy cream

1 cup unsweetened almond milk

1/3 cup erythritol

Juice and zest of 2 lemons

For Blueberry Layer:

1 cup blueberries (fresh or frozen)

1/4 cup erythritol

For the Crust:

1 1/2 cups almond flour

1/4 cup coconut oil, melted

2 tbsp erythritol

M.C.: Freezing

Procedure:

Crust: Combine almond flour, coconut oil, and erythritol. Press into the bottom of a springform pan. Freeze for 20 minutes.

Lemon Ice Cream: Mix heavy cream,

almond milk, erythritol, lemon juice, and zest. Pour over crust and freeze for 2 hours.

Blueberry Layer: Blend blueberries with erythritol. Spread over lemon layer. Freeze until set.

N.V.: Estimated per serving: Calories: 270, Fat: 23g, Carbs: 7g (net), Protein: 3g.

milk, and erythritol. Pour over crust, freeze for 2 hours.

Fudge Layer: Melt coconut oil with cocoa powder and erythritol. Pour over coffee layer. Freeze until set.

N.V.: Estimated per serving: Calories: 290, Fat: 25g, Carbs: 8g (net), Protein: 4g.

Recipe 6: Coffee Almond Fudge Ice Cream Cake

P.T.: 5 hours (including freezing time)

Ingr:

For Coffee Ice Cream Layer:

2 cups heavy cream

1 cup unsweetened almond milk

1/3 cup erythritol

2 tbsp instant coffee granules

For Fudge Layer:

1/4 cup unsweetened cocoa powder

1/4 cup coconut oil

1/4 cup erythritol

For the Crust:

1 1/2 cups almond flour

1/4 cup coconut oil, melted

2 tbsp erythritol

M.C.: Freezing

Procedure:

Crust: Mix almond flour with coconut oil and erythritol, press into a springform pan. Freeze for 20 minutes.

Coffee Ice Cream: Dissolve instant coffee in a little hot water. Mix with cream, almond

Recipe 7: Raspberry Ripple Ice Cream Cake

P.T.: 6 hours (including freezing time)

Ingr:

For Vanilla Ice Cream Base:

2 cups heavy cream

1 cup unsweetened almond milk

1/3 cup erythritol

1 tsp vanilla extract

For Raspberry Swirl:

1 cup raspberries (fresh or frozen)

1/4 cup erythritol

For the Crust:

1 1/2 cups almond flour

1/4 cup butter, melted

2 tbsp erythritol

M.C.: Freezing

Procedure:

Crust: Combine almond flour, melted butter, and erythritol. Press into a springform pan. Freeze for 20 minutes.

Vanilla Ice Cream: Whip cream, almond milk, erythritol, and vanilla. Pour over crust. Freeze for 1 hour.

Raspberry Swirl: Puree raspberries with erythritol. Swirl into semi-frozen vanilla base. Freeze until firm.

N.V.: Estimated per serving: Calories: 280, Fat: 24g, Carbs: 8g (net), Protein: 4g.

Chapter 8: Festive Desserts for Special Occasions

Elegant Desserts for Formal Gatherings

Recipe 1: Raspberry Almond Frangipane Tart

P.T.: 1 hour 15 minutes

Ingr:

For the crust: 1 1/2 cups almond flour, 1/4 cup coconut flour, 1/4 cup unsalted butter (melted), 1 egg.

For the filling: 1 cup almond meal, 1/2 cup erythritol, 1/2 cup unsalted butter (softened), 2 eggs, 1 tsp almond extract, 1 cup fresh raspberries.

M.C.: Baking

Procedure:

Preheat the oven to 350°F (175°C). Mix crust ingredients and press into a tart pan. Bake for 10 minutes.

Cream together the butter and erythritol for the filling. Add eggs, almond meal, and almond extract. Spread over the pre-baked crust.

Press raspberries into the filling. Bake for 35-40 minutes until set.

N.V.: Estimated per serving: Calories: 280, Fat: 25g, Carbs: 8g (net), Protein: 6g.

Recipe 2: Chocolate Avocado Mousse with Hazelnut Crunch

P.T.: 15 minutes + chilling

Ingr:

2 ripe avocados, 1/2 cup unsweetened cocoa powder, 1/3 cup erythritol, 1 tsp vanilla extract, 1/4 cup almond milk.

For the crunch: 1/2 cup chopped hazelnuts, 2 tbsp erythritol.

M.C.: Mixing/Chilling

Procedure:

Blend avocados, cocoa powder, erythritol, vanilla extract, and almond milk until smooth.

Toast hazelnuts with erythritol until caramelized. Cool and chop finely.

Layer mousse with hazelnut crunch in serving glasses. Chill before serving.

N.V.: Estimated per serving: Calories: 220, Fat: 18g, Carbs: 10g (net), Protein: 4g.

Recipe 3: Lemon Lavender Panna Cotta

P.T.: 4 hours (including setting time)

Ingr:

2 cups heavy cream (or coconut cream for dairy-free), 1/4 cup erythritol, Zest of 1 lemon, 1 tbsp dried lavender, 2 tsp gelatin powder, 1/4 cup water.

M.C.: Simmering/Chilling

Procedure:

Sprinkle gelatin over water; let bloom. Heat cream with erythritol, lemon zest, and lavender until hot but not boiling. Remove from heat; add gelatin, stirring until dissolved.

Strain mixture to remove lavender and zest. Pour into molds. Chill until set.

N.V.: Estimated per serving: Calories: 250, Fat: 24g, Carbs: 4g (net), Protein: 3g.

Recipe 4: Keto Opera Cake

P.T.: 2 hours

Ingr:

For almond sponge cake: 1 cup almond flour, 1/3 cup erythritol, 4 eggs (separated), 1 tsp vanilla extract.

For coffee buttercream: 1 cup unsalted butter (softened), 1/4 cup erythritol, 2 tbsp strong brewed coffee.

For chocolate ganache: 1/2 cup heavy cream, 1/2 cup sugar-free dark chocolate chips.

M.C.: Baking/Assembling

Procedure:

Bake almond sponge cake; cool and slice into layers. Whip buttercream with coffee; spread between cake layers.

Heat cream; pour over chocolate chips for ganache. Spread over assembled cake. Chill to set.

N.V.: Estimated per serving: Calories: 310, Fat: 28g, Carbs: 6g (net), Protein: 5g.

Recipe 5: Saffron and Cardamom Infused Berry Compote over Greek Yogurt

P.T.: 20 minutes + chilling

Ingr:

1 cup mixed berries, 1/4 cup water, 1/4 cup erythritol, 1 tsp lemon juice, A pinch of saffron threads, 1/2 tsp ground cardamom, 2 cups Greek yogurt (unsweetened).

M.C.: Simmering

Procedure:

Simmer berries, water, erythritol, lemon juice, saffron, and cardamom until berries are soft and syrup forms.

Cool the compote. Serve over Greek yogurt.

N.V.: Estimated per serving: Calories: 120, Fat: 4g, Carbs: 8g (net), Protein: 15g.

Recipe 6: Keto Tiramisu

P.T.: 1 hour + chilling

Ingr:

For the cake: 1 cup almond flour, 1/3 cup erythritol, 4 eggs, 1 tsp vanilla extract.

For the filling: 1 cup mascarpone cheese, 1/4 cup erythritol, 1/2 cup strong brewed coffee (cooled), Unsweetened cocoa powder for dusting.

M.C.: Baking/Assembling

Procedure:

Bake almond flour cake, slice into thin layers. Mix mascarpone with erythritol.

Dip cake layers in coffee, layer with mascarpone mixture. Dust with cocoa. Chill to set.

N.V.: Estimated per serving: Calories: 320, Fat: 28g, Carbs: 5g (net), Protein: 8g.

Recipe 7: Pistachio Rosewater Pavlova

P.T.: 2 hours (including baking and cooling time)

Ingr:

For the pavlova: 4 egg whites, 1/4 cup erythritol, 1 tsp white vinegar, 1 tsp cornstarch, 1/2 cup crushed pistachios.

For the topping: 1 cup heavy whipping cream, 2 tbsp erythritol, 1 tsp rosewater, Fresh raspberries for garnish.

M.C.: Baking/Whipping

Procedure:

Beat egg whites to soft peaks, gradually add erythritol, vinegar, and cornstarch. Fold in pistachios. Shape into a circle on a baking sheet; bake at low heat until crisp.

Whip cream with erythritol and rosewater. Top pavlova with cream and raspberries.

N.V.: Estimated per serving: Calories: 220, Fat: 18g, Carbs: 8g (net), Protein: 4g.

Holiday Treats Everyone Can Enjoy

Recipe 1: Gingerbread Keto Cookies

P.T.: 45 minutes

Ingr:

2 cups almond flour

1/4 cup coconut flour

1/3 cup erythritol

2 tsp ginger, ground

1 tsp cinnamon, ground

1/4 tsp nutmeg, ground

1/4 tsp cloves, ground

1/2 tsp baking powder

1/4 cup unsalted butter, melted

1 egg

1/4 cup sugar-free syrup

M.C.: Baking

Procedure:

Preheat oven to 350°F (175°C) and line a baking sheet with parchment paper.

Mix dry ingredients in a large bowl. Stir in melted butter, egg, and syrup until dough forms.

Roll out dough between two pieces of parchment paper, cut into gingerbread shapes.

Place on prepared baking sheet, bake for 10-12 minutes until edges are slightly golden.

N.V.: Estimated per cookie: Calories: 130, Fat: 11g, Carbs: 3g (net), Protein: 4g.

Recipe 2: Pumpkin Spice Cheesecake Bites

P.T.: 2 hours (includes chilling)

Ingr:

For the crust: 1 cup almond flour, 2 tbsp erythritol, 1/4 cup butter, melted.

For the filling: 1 cup cream cheese, softened, 1/2 cup pumpkin puree, 1/4 cup erythritol, 1 tsp vanilla extract, 2 tsp pumpkin pie spice.

M.C.: No-bake

Procedure:

Mix crust ingredients, press into the bottom of a lined mini muffin pan. Chill for 20 minutes.

Beat filling ingredients until smooth. Spoon over crusts.

Freeze until set, about 1.5 hours. Serve chilled.

N.V.: Estimated per bite: Calories: 100, Fat: 9g, Carbs: 2g (net), Protein: 2g.

Recipe 3: Sugar-Free Peppermint Mocha Truffles

P.T.: 1 hour (includes chilling)

Ingr:

1/2 cup heavy cream

1/4 cup erythritol

1/2 tsp peppermint extract

1 cup sugar-free dark chocolate chips

1 tsp instant coffee granules

Cocoa powder for dusting

M.C.: Melting/Chilling

Procedure:

Heat cream and erythritol until simmering. Remove from heat, add chocolate chips, coffee, and peppermint. Stir until smooth.

Chill mixture until firm. Roll into balls and dust with cocoa powder.

N.V.: Estimated per truffle: Calories: 60, Fat: 5g, Carbs: 1g (net), Protein: 1g.

Recipe 4: Holiday Spiced Nut Mix

P.T.: 30 minutes

Ingr:

2 cups mixed nuts (almonds, pecans, walnuts)

1/4 cup erythritol

1 egg white

1 tsp water

1 tsp cinnamon

1/2 tsp nutmeg

1/4 tsp cloves

M.C.: Baking

Procedure:

Whisk egg white and water until frothy. Add nuts and erythritol, toss to coat.

Sprinkle with spices, toss again. Spread on a baking sheet.

Bake at 300°F (150°C) for 20 minutes, stirring halfway through.

N.V.: Estimated per serving: Calories: 160, Fat: 14g, Carbs: 4g (net), Protein: 5g.

Recipe 5: Eggnog Panna Cotta

P.T.: 4 hours (includes setting)

Ingr:

2 cups almond milk

1 cup heavy cream

1/4 cup erythritol

2 tsp gelatin powder

1/2 tsp nutmeg

1 tsp vanilla extract

1/4 cup rum or brandy (optional)

M.C.: Simmering/Chilling

Procedure:

Sprinkle gelatin over a portion of almond milk. Let bloom.

Heat remaining almond milk, cream, erythritol, and nutmeg until hot. Add gelatin mixture, vanilla, and alcohol if using.

Pour into molds, chill until set.

N.V.: Estimated per serving: Calories: 180, Fat: 16g, Carbs: 3g (net), Protein: 3g.

Recipe 6: Cranberry Orange Relish

P.T.: 15 minutes

Ingr:

2 cups fresh cranberries

Zest and juice of 1 orange

1/4 cup erythritol

1/2 cup water

M.C.: Simmering

Procedure:

Combine all ingredients in a saucepan.

Simmer over medium heat until cranberries burst and mixture thickens.

Cool completely before serving.

N.V.: Estimated per serving: Calories: 25, Fat: 0g, Carbs: 6g (net), Protein: 0g.

Recipe 7: Low-Carb Yule Log

P.T.: 1 hour 30 minutes

Ingr:

For the cake: 6 eggs (separated), 1/3 cup erythritol, 1/4 cup almond flour, 1/4 cup cocoa powder, 1 tsp vanilla extract.

For the filling: 1 cup heavy cream, 1/4 cup

erythritol, 1 tsp vanilla extract.

For the frosting: 1 cup sugar-free dark chocolate chips, 1/2 cup heavy cream.

M.C.: Baking/Assembling

Procedure:

Beat egg whites to stiff peaks. Mix yolks with erythritol, almond flour, cocoa, and vanilla.

Fold in egg whites.

Bake in a lined jelly roll pan. Roll, cool, then fill with whipped cream.

Frost with melted chocolate and cream mixture. Chill before serving.

N.V.: Estimated per serving: Calories: 220, Fat: 18g, Carbs: 5g (net), Protein: 6g.

Celebratory Cakes without the Sugar Crash

Recipe 1: Almond Joy Layer Cake

P.T.: 1 hour 30 minutes

Ingr:

For the cake: 3 cups almond flour, 1 cup erythritol, 1 tsp baking soda, 1/2 tsp salt, 4 eggs, 1 cup unsweetened coconut milk, 1 tsp vanilla extract.

For the filling: 1 cup unsweetened shredded coconut, 1/2 cup chopped almonds, 1/4 cup erythritol, 1/4 cup coconut cream.

For the frosting: 2 cups heavy cream, 1/2 cup erythritol, 1/2 cup unsweetened cocoa powder.

M.C.: Baking

Procedure:

Mix dry cake ingredients, then add wet ingredients. Pour into two greased cake pans, bake at 350°F (175°C) for 25-30 minutes.

For filling, mix coconut, almonds, erythritol,

and coconut cream. Spread between cooled cake layers.

Whip heavy cream, erythritol, and cocoa for frosting. Frost cake.

N.V.: Estimated per serving: Calories: 320, Fat: 28g, Carbs: 8g (net), Protein: 9g.

Recipe 2: Lemon Raspberry Cheesecake

P.T.: 4 hours (including chilling)

Ingr:

For the crust: 1 1/2 cups almond flour, 1/4 cup erythritol, 1/3 cup butter, melted.

For the filling: 3 cups cream cheese, softened, 1 cup erythritol, zest and juice of 2 lemons, 1 tsp vanilla extract, 1 cup raspberries.

M.C.: No-bake

Procedure:

Mix crust ingredients, press into a springform pan, chill.

Beat filling ingredients (except raspberries) until smooth. Fold in raspberries. Pour over crust, chill until set.

N.V.: Estimated per serving: Calories: 300, Fat: 27g, Carbs: 6g (net), Protein: 7g.

Recipe 3: Classic Keto Vanilla Cake

P.T.: 1 hour

Ingr:

2 1/2 cups almond flour, 1/2 cup erythritol, 1/4 cup coconut flour, 1 tsp baking powder, 1/2 tsp salt, 5 eggs, 1 cup unsweetened almond milk, 1 tbsp vanilla extract, 1/2 cup unsalted butter, melted.

M.C.: Baking

Procedure:

Combine dry ingredients. In another bowl, mix eggs, almond milk, vanilla, and melted butter. Combine with dry ingredients, pour into a greased cake pan, and bake at 350°F (175°C) for 35 minutes.

N.V.: Estimated per serving: Calories: 260, Fat: 22g, Carbs: 5g (net), Protein: 8g.

Recipe 4: Chocolate Hazelnut Torte

P.T.: 1 hour 15 minutes

Ingr:

2 cups hazelnut meal, 1/2 cup erythritol, 1/4 cup unsweetened cocoa powder, 1 tsp baking powder, 6 eggs, separated, 1/2 cup unsalted butter, melted, 1 tsp vanilla extract.

M.C.: Baking

Procedure:

Whisk egg whites to stiff peaks. Mix hazelnut meal, erythritol, cocoa, and baking powder. Stir in yolks, butter, vanilla. Fold in egg whites. Bake in a greased pan at 350°F (175°C) for 40 minutes.

N.V.: Estimated per serving: Calories: 280, Fat: 25g, Carbs: 3g (net), Protein: 9g.

Recipe 5: Strawberries and Cream Sponge Cake

P.T.: 1 hour 30 minutes

Ingr:

For the cake: 2 cups almond flour, 1/2 cup erythritol, 1 tsp baking powder, 6 eggs, separated, 1/4 cup unsweetened almond milk, 1 tsp vanilla extract.

For the filling and topping: 2 cups sliced strawberries, 2 cups heavy cream, 1/4 cup erythritol.

M.C.: Baking

Procedure:

Beat egg whites to stiff peaks. Mix almond flour, erythritol, baking powder. Add yolks, almond milk, vanilla. Fold in egg whites. Bake at 350°F (175°C) for 25 minutes. Cool and slice horizontally.

Whip cream and erythritol to stiff peaks. Layer cake with cream and strawberries.

N.V.: Estimated per serving: Calories: 310, Fat: 27g, Carbs: 7g (net), Protein: 8g.

Recipe 6: Spiced Carrot Cake with Cream Cheese Frosting

P.T.: 1 hour 30 minutes

Ingr:

For the cake: 2 cups almond flour, 1/2 cup coconut flour, 1/2 cup erythritol, 2 tsp cinnamon, 1 tsp nutmeg, 1/2 tsp ginger, 1/2 tsp salt, 4 eggs, 1/2 cup coconut oil, melted, 2 cups grated carrots.

For the frosting: 1 cup cream cheese, softened, 1/4 cup butter, softened, 1/4 cup erythritol, 1 tsp vanilla extract.

M.C.: Baking

Procedure:

Mix dry cake ingredients, then wet ingredients, and combine. Stir in carrots. Pour into pans, bake at 350°F (175°C) for 30 minutes.

Beat frosting ingredients until smooth. Frost cooled cake.

N.V.: Estimated per serving: Calories: 320, Fat: 28g, Carbs: 8g (net), Protein: 7g.

Recipe 7: Keto Black Forest Cake

P.T.: 2 hours

Ingr:

For the cake: 2 cups almond flour, 1/2 cup erythritol, 1/4 cup unsweetened cocoa powder, 1 tsp baking soda, 1/2 tsp salt, 4 eggs, 1/2 cup unsweetened almond milk, 1/4 cup unsalted butter, melted, 1 tsp vanilla extract.

For the filling: 1 cup sugar-free cherry pie filling.

For the frosting: 2 cups heavy cream, 1/4 cup erythritol, 1 tsp vanilla extract.

M.C.: Baking

Procedure:

Mix cake ingredients, bake in two rounds at 350°F (175°C) for 25 minutes. Cool.

Whip cream, erythritol, and vanilla for frosting.

Assemble cake with cherry filling between layers and frosted.

N.V.: Estimated per serving: Calories: 330, Fat: 29g, Carbs: 9g (net), Protein: 8g.

Chapter 9: International Desserts with a Diabetic Twist

European Delights with a Healthy Twist

Recipe 1: Keto Tiramisu

P.T.: 1 hour + chilling time

Ingr:

For the sponge: Almond flour, erythritol, eggs, espresso.

For the filling: Mascarpone cheese, heavy cream, erythritol, vanilla extract.

M.C.: Layering/Refrigerating

Procedure:

Bake a low-carb almond flour sponge cake, slice thinly.

Mix mascarpone with erythritol and vanilla, fold in whipped heavy cream.

Dip sponge slices in espresso, layer with mascarpone cream. Chill until set.

N.V.: Focus on low-carb, high-fat content suitable for a keto diet.

Recipe 2: French Lemon Tart with Almond Crust

P.T.: 1 hour 30 minutes

Ingr:

For the crust: Almond flour, butter, erythritol.

For the filling: Eggs, erythritol, fresh lemon juice, lemon zest.

M.C.: Baking

Procedure:

Prepare an almond flour crust and pre-bake.

Mix filling ingredients, pour into crust, and bake until set.

N.V.: Emphasize the high fiber from almonds and low-carb sweetener.

Recipe 3: Spanish Almond Cake

P.T.: 50 minutes

Ingr:

Ground almonds, erythritol, eggs, lemon zest, cinnamon.

M.C.: Baking

Procedure:

Beat eggs with erythritol and lemon zest until fluffy.

Fold in ground almonds and cinnamon, bake until golden.

N.V.: Highlight the protein and healthy fats from almonds, with minimal carbs.

Recipe 4: Keto Black Forest Cake

P.T.: 2 hours

Ingr:

Almond flour, unsweetened cocoa powder, erythritol, eggs, cherry extract, unsweetened cherries, whipped cream.

M.C.: Baking/Assembling

Procedure:

Bake chocolate almond flour cakes.

Layer with whipped cream and cherries, flavored with cherry extract.

N.V.: Low-carb, using sugar alternatives and focusing on healthy fats.

Recipe 5: Italian Ricotta Cheesecake

P.T.: 1 hour + chilling time

Ingr:

Ricotta cheese, erythritol, eggs, almond flour, lemon zest.

M.C.: Baking

Procedure:

Mix ricotta with erythritol, lemon zest, and eggs.

Pour into an almond flour crust, bake until set. Chill before serving.

N.V.: Low in carbs, high in protein, using natural sweeteners.

Recipe 6: Austrian Linzer Torte

P.T.: 1 hour 30 minutes

Ingr:

For the dough: Almond flour, butter, erythritol, egg, cinnamon, lemon zest.

For the filling: Sugar-free raspberry jam.

M.C.: Baking

Procedure:

Prepare dough, press into tart pan, fill with jam.

Add lattice top, bake until golden.

N.V.: Focus on the use of almond flour and sugar-free jam for a low-carb dessert.

Recipe 7: Greek Yogurt Panna Cotta

P.T.: 4 hours (including setting time)

Ingr:

Greek yogurt, erythritol, vanilla bean, gelatin, almond milk.

M.C.: Simmering/Chilling

Procedure:

Dissolve gelatin in almond milk, mix with sweetened Greek yogurt.

Pour into molds, chill until set. Serve with sugar-free berry compote.

N.V.: High in protein, low in carbs, enriched with probiotics from yogurt.

Asian-Inspired Sugar-Free Sweets

Recipe 1: Keto Matcha Green Tea Cheesecake

P.T.: 2 hours (including chilling)

Ingr:

For the crust: 1 cup almond flour, 1/4 cup unsalted butter (melted), 1 tbsp erythritol.

For the filling: 2 cups cream cheese (softened), 1/2 cup erythritol, 2 tbsp matcha green tea powder, 1 cup heavy cream, 1 tsp vanilla extract.

M.C.: No-bake

Procedure:

Mix crust ingredients and press into the bottom of a springform pan. Chill.

Beat filling ingredients until smooth and pour over the crust. Refrigerate until set.

N.V.: Calories: 320, Fat: 30g, Net Carbs: 5g, Protein: 6g.

Recipe 2: Sugar-Free Coconut Milk Mango Mochi

P.T.: 1 hour

Ingr:

1 cup coconut flour, 1/4 cup erythritol, 1 can (14 oz) coconut milk, 1 tsp vanilla extract, 1 ripe mango (diced), Coconut flakes for coating.

M.C.: Steaming

Procedure:

Mix coconut flour, erythritol, coconut milk, and vanilla to form a dough.

Divide the dough, fill with mango pieces, form into balls.

Steam for 15 minutes, roll in coconut flakes.

N.V.: Calories: 150, Fat: 9g, Net Carbs: 8g, Protein: 2g.

Recipe 3: Keto Sesame Seed Balls (Jian Dui)

P.T.: 45 minutes

Ingr:

1 cup almond flour, 1/2 cup sesame seeds, 1/4 cup erythritol, 1 egg, Water as needed, 1/4 cup sugar-free red bean paste.

M.C.: Frying

Procedure:

Mix almond flour and erythritol, add egg and water to form a dough.

Wrap dough around red bean paste, form balls, roll in sesame seeds.

Fry in oil until golden.

N.V.: Calories: 200, Fat: 15g, Net Carbs: 3g, Protein: 6g.

Recipe 4: Diabetic-Friendly Sweet Potato Mooncakes

P.T.: 2 hours

Ingr:

For the crust: 2 cups almond flour, 1/4 cup erythritol, 1/4 cup unsalted butter, 1 egg.

For the filling: 1 large sweet potato (steamed and mashed), 1 tbsp erythritol, 1 tsp cinnamon.

M.C.: Baking

Procedure:

Prepare the crust dough, chill. Mix filling ingredients.

Fill crust with sweet potato mixture, shape using mooncake mold.

Bake at 350°F (175°C) for 20 minutes.

N.V.: Calories: 280, Fat: 22g, Net Carbs: 8g, Protein: 7g.

Recipe 5: Sugar-Free Lychee Jelly

P.T.: 3 hours (including setting)

Ingr:

2 cups water, 1/4 cup erythritol, 1 cup lychee (pitted and chopped), 2 tbsp gelatin powder.

M.C.: Boiling/Chilling

Procedure:

Dissolve erythritol and gelatin in boiling water.

Add chopped lychee, pour into molds, chill until set.

N.V.: Calories: 50, Fat: 0g, Net Carbs: 4g, Protein: 2g.

Recipe 6: Keto Almond Jelly (Annin Tofu)

P.T.: 2 hours (including chilling)

Ingr:

2 cups almond milk, 1/4 cup erythritol, 2 tsp almond extract, 2 tbsp gelatin powder, Sliced almonds for garnish.

M.C.: Boiling/Chilling

Procedure:

Dissolve gelatin and erythritol in almond milk over low heat.

Stir in almond extract, pour into molds, chill until set. Garnish with almonds.

N.V.: Calories: 60, Fat: 4g, Net Carbs: 1g, Protein: 5g.

Recipe 7: Sugar-Free Matcha Ice Cream

P.T.: 4 hours (including freezing)

Ingr:

1 can (14 oz) full-fat coconut milk, 1/4 cup erythritol, 2 tbsp matcha powder, 1 tsp vanilla extract.

M.C.: Freezing

Procedure:

Whisk together coconut milk, erythritol, matcha, and vanilla.

Freeze in an ice cream maker or stir every 30 minutes in the freezer until set.

N.V.: Calories: 200, Fat: 18g, Net Carbs: 2g, Protein: 2g.

Middle Eastern Desserts for Diabetic Diets

Recipe 1: Keto Baklava Bites

P.T.: 1 hour

Ingr:

1 cup almond flour

1/2 cup chopped walnuts

1/4 cup unsalted butter, melted

2 tbsp erythritol

1 tsp cinnamon

For the syrup: 1/4 cup water, 1/4 cup erythritol, 1 tsp lemon juice, 1/2 tsp rose water

M.C.: Baking

Procedure:

Mix almond flour, walnuts, erythritol, and cinnamon. Layer with melted butter in mini muffin tins.

Bake at 350°F (175°C) for 20 minutes. Meanwhile, simmer the syrup ingredients until thickened.

Pour syrup over baked bites. Cool before serving.

N.V.: Calories: 80, Fat: 7g, Net Carbs: 2g, Protein: 2g.

Recipe 2: Sugar-Free Pistachio Halva

P.T.: 30 minutes + chilling

Ingr:

2 cups fine almond flour

1 cup erythritol

1/2 cup unsalted butter

1/2 cup finely ground pistachios

1 tsp cardamom powder

M.C.: Stovetop

Procedure:

Melt butter over low heat, stir in erythritol until dissolved.

Add almond flour and cardamom, cook until golden. Stir in pistachios.

Press into a pan, chill until set. Slice into squares.

N.V.: Calories: 100, Fat: 9g, Net Carbs: 2g, Protein: 3g.

Recipe 3: Low-Carb Rosewater and Saffron Mousse

P.T.: 2 hours (including chilling)

Ingr:

1 cup heavy whipping cream

1/4 cup erythritol

A pinch of saffron threads

1 tsp rosewater

Pistachios for garnish

M.C.: Whipping/Chilling

Procedure:

Infuse saffron in 2 tbsp hot water. Whip cream with erythritol to soft peaks.

Fold in saffron water and rosewater. Spoon into serving glasses.

Chill until set. Garnish with pistachios.

N.V.: Calories: 120, Fat: 11g, Net Carbs: 3g, Protein: 1g.

Recipe 4: Keto Date and Walnut Bars

P.T.: 45 minutes

Ingr:

1 cup chopped dates (sugar-free or very low sugar)

1 cup walnuts

1 cup almond flour

1/4 cup unsalted butter, melted

1 tsp cinnamon

M.C.: Baking

Procedure:

Process dates and walnuts until combined. Mix with almond flour, melted butter, and cinnamon.

Press into a lined baking dish. Bake at 350°F (175°C) for 25 minutes.

Cool before slicing into bars.

N.V.: Calories: 150, Fat: 12g, Net Carbs: 4g, Protein: 3g.

Recipe 5: Almond and Orange Flourless Cake

P.T.: 1 hour

Ingr:

2 cups ground almonds

1 cup erythritol

3 eggs

Zest and juice of 1 orange

1 tsp baking powder

M.C.: Baking

Procedure:

Beat eggs with erythritol until fluffy. Fold in ground almonds, orange zest, juice, and baking powder.

Pour into a greased cake pan. Bake at 350°F (175°C) for 35 minutes.

Cool before serving.

N.V.: Calories: 200, Fat: 17g, Net Carbs: 3g, Protein: 6g.

Recipe 6: Sugar-Free Lebanese Nights (Layali Lubnan)

P.T.: 2 hours (including chilling)

Ingr:

2 cups almond milk

1/4 cup erythritol

1/4 cup coconut flour

2 tbsp orange blossom water

Pistachios and dried rose petals for garnish

M.C.: Stovetop

Procedure:

Whisk almond milk, erythritol, and coconut

flour over medium heat until thickened.

Stir in orange blossom water. Pour into a dish, chill until set.

Garnish with pistachios and rose petals before serving.

N.V.: Calories: 100, Fat: 8g, Net Carbs: 4g, Protein: 2g.

Recipe 7: Creamy Cardamom Rose Flavored Yogurt

P.T.: 15 minutes + chilling

Ingr:

2 cups Greek yogurt (unsweetened)

1/4 cup erythritol

1 tsp ground cardamom

1 tsp rosewater

Slivered almonds and rose petals for garnish

M.C.: Mixing/Chilling

Procedure:

Mix yogurt with erythritol, cardamom, and rosewater until smooth.

Chill for at least 1 hour. Garnish with slivered almonds and rose petals before serving.

N.V.: Calories: 120, Fat: 6g, Net Carbs: 5g, Protein: 12g.

Chapter 10: Sweets for Gestational Diabetes

Nutrient-Rich Snacks for Expecting Mothers

Recipe 1: Avocado and Egg Salad Cups

P.T.: 20 minutes

Ingr:

2 ripe avocados, halved and pitted

4 hard-boiled eggs, chopped

1/4 cup Greek yogurt, unsweetened

2 tbsp chives, finely chopped

Salt and pepper to taste

Paprika for garnish

M.C.: Mixing/Assembling

Procedure:

Scoop out some avocado flesh to make room for the filling, mash the scooped avocado.

Mix chopped eggs, mashed avocado, Greek yogurt, and chives. Season with salt and pepper.

Fill avocado halves with the egg salad mixture. Sprinkle with paprika.

N.V.: Calories: 250, Fat: 20g, Net Carbs: 6g, Protein: 12g.

Recipe 2: Spinach and Feta Stuffed Mushrooms

P.T.: 30 minutes

Ingr:

12 large button mushrooms, stems removed

1 cup spinach, chopped

1/2 cup feta cheese, crumbled

2 cloves garlic, minced

1 tbsp olive oil

Salt and pepper to taste

M.C.: Baking

Procedure:

Preheat oven to 375°F (190°C). Sauté spinach and garlic in olive oil until wilted.

Mix spinach with feta cheese, season with salt and pepper.

Stuff mushrooms with the spinach mixture. Bake for 15-20 minutes.

N.V.: Calories: 60, Fat: 4g, Net Carbs: 2g, Protein: 3g.

Recipe 3: Greek Yogurt and Berry Parfait

P.T.: 10 minutes

Ingr:

1 cup Greek yogurt, unsweetened

1/2 cup mixed berries (strawberries, blueberries, raspberries)

1/4 cup granola (low-carb, sugar-free)

1 tbsp almond slivers

M.C.: Layering

Procedure:

In a glass or jar, layer Greek yogurt, mixed berries, and granola.

Repeat the layers until ingredients are used up.

Top with almond slivers.

N.V.: Calories: 180, Fat: 9g, Net Carbs: 8g, Protein: 15g.

Recipe 4: Quinoa and Black Bean Salad

P.T.: 25 minutes

Ingr:

1 cup cooked quinoa, cooled

1/2 cup black beans, rinsed and drained

1/2 cup corn kernels

1/2 cup cherry tomatoes, halved

1/4 cup red onion, finely chopped

2 tbsp cilantro, chopped

Juice of 1 lime

1 tbsp olive oil

Salt and pepper to taste

M.C.: Mixing

Procedure:

In a large bowl, combine quinoa, black beans, corn, cherry tomatoes, and red onion. Add lime juice, olive oil, cilantro, salt, and pepper. Toss to combine.

N.V.: Calories: 200, Fat: 5g, Net Carbs: 30g, Protein: 8g.

Recipe 5: Almond Butter and Banana Smoothie

P.T.: 5 minutes

Ingr:

1 medium banana, sliced and frozen

2 tbsp almond butter

1 cup almond milk, unsweetened

1/2 tsp cinnamon

1 scoop protein powder (optional)

M.C.: Blending

Procedure:

Combine all ingredients in a blender.

Blend until smooth and creamy.

N.V.: Calories: 320, Fat: 18g, Net Carbs: 24g, Protein: 10g (varies with protein powder).

Recipe 6: Cottage Cheese and Peach Compote

P.T.: 15 minutes

Ingr:

1 cup cottage cheese

1 peach, sliced

1/4 cup water

1 tbsp erythritol

1/2 tsp vanilla extract

M.C.: Simmering/Assembling

Procedure:

Simmer peach slices, water, erythritol, and vanilla in a small saucepan until peaches are soft. Let cool slightly, then serve over cottage cheese.

N.V.: Calories: 150, Fat: 2g, Net Carbs: 10g, Protein: 14g.

Recipe 7: Chia Seed and Coconut Milk Pudding

P.T.: 4 hours (including setting)

Ingr:

1/4 cup chia seeds

1 cup coconut milk, unsweetened

1 tbsp erythritol

1/2 tsp vanilla extract

Fresh berries for topping

M.C.: Mixing/Refrigerating

Procedure:

Mix chia seeds, coconut milk, erythritol, and vanilla extract in a bowl.

Refrigerate for at least 4 hours or overnight until set.

Top with fresh berries before serving.

N.V.: Calories: 200, Fat: 15g, Net Carbs: 5g, Protein: 3g.

Quick and Easy Meals for Busy Moms-to-Be

Recipe 1: Turkey and Quinoa Stuffed Peppers

P.T.: 45 minutes

Ingr:

4 bell peppers, halved and deseeded

1 lb ground turkey

1 cup cooked quinoa

1 cup spinach, chopped

1/2 cup tomato sauce (sugar-free)

1/4 cup feta cheese, crumbled

1 tsp garlic powder

1 tsp olive oil

Salt and pepper to taste

M.C.: Baking

Procedure:

Preheat oven to 375°F (190°C). Sauté ground turkey in olive oil until cooked. Mix in quinoa, spinach, tomato sauce, garlic powder, salt, and pepper.

Stuff the mixture into bell pepper halves, top with feta cheese.

Bake for 25 minutes until peppers are tender.

N.V.: Calories: 220, Fat: 8g, Carbs: 15g, Protein: 20g.

Recipe 2: Spinach and Mushroom Frittata

P.T.: 30 minutes

Ingr:

6 eggs

1 cup fresh spinach

1/2 cup mushrooms, sliced

1/4 cup cheddar cheese, grated

1/4 cup milk (or almond milk)

1 tbsp olive oil

Salt and pepper to taste

M.C.: Baking

Procedure:

Preheat oven to 350°F (175°C). In a skillet, sauté mushrooms in olive oil until soft. Add spinach until wilted.

Whisk eggs, milk, salt, and pepper. Stir in sautéed vegetables and cheese.

Pour into a greased baking dish. Bake for 20 minutes until set.

N.V.: Calories: 150, Fat: 10g, Carbs: 2g, Protein: 12g.

Recipe 3: Avocado Chicken Salad

P.T.: 15 minutes

Ingr:

2 cups cooked chicken breast, shredded

1 ripe avocado, mashed

1/4 cup Greek yogurt, unsweetened

1/2 cup celery, diced

1/4 cup red onion, minced

1 tbsp lemon juice

Salt and pepper to taste

M.C.: Mixing

Procedure:

In a large bowl, combine all ingredients thoroughly.

Serve chilled on whole grain or low-carb

bread, or over a bed of greens.

N.V.: Calories: 210, Fat: 9g, Carbs: 6g, Protein: 25g.

Recipe 4: Salmon and Asparagus One-Pan Dinner

P.T.: 25 minutes

Ingr:

4 salmon fillets

1 lb asparagus, ends trimmed

2 tbsp olive oil

2 garlic cloves, minced

1 lemon, sliced

Salt and pepper to taste

M.C.: Roasting

Procedure:

Preheat oven to 400°F (200°C). Place salmon and asparagus on a baking sheet.

Drizzle with olive oil, sprinkle with garlic, salt, and pepper. Top with lemon slices.

Roast for 15-20 minutes, until salmon is cooked through.

N.V.: Calories: 300, Fat: 18g, Carbs: 5g, Protein: 30g.

Recipe 5: Zucchini Noodles with Pesto Chicken

P.T.: 20 minutes

Ingr:

2 large zucchinis, spiralized

1 lb chicken breast, cooked and shredded

1/2 cup pesto sauce (sugar-free)

1 tbsp olive oil

Salt and pepper to taste

Parmesan cheese, for garnish (optional)

M.C.: Sautéing

Procedure:

Heat olive oil in a pan. Add spiralized zucchini, sauté for 3-5 minutes until tender. Stir in shredded chicken and pesto sauce. Cook until heated through.

Serve with a sprinkle of Parmesan if desired.

N.V.: Calories: 280, Fat: 16g, Carbs: 6g, Protein: 28g.

Recipe 6: Quick Veggie Stir-Fry with Tofu

P.T.: 20 minutes

Ingr:

1 lb firm tofu, cubed

2 cups mixed vegetables (bell peppers, broccoli, snap peas)

2 tbsp soy sauce (low sodium)

1 tbsp sesame oil

1 garlic clove, minced

1 tsp ginger, grated

M.C.: Stir-frying

Procedure:

Heat sesame oil in a wok or large pan. Add garlic and ginger, sauté for 1 minute.

Add tofu, cook until golden. Add vegetables, stir-fry until crisp-tender.

Stir in soy sauce, cook for another 2 minutes.

N.V.: Calories: 180, Fat: 10g, Carbs: 8g, Protein: 16g.

Recipe 7: Beef and Broccoli Bowl

P.T.: 30 minutes

Ingr:

1 lb lean beef, thinly sliced

2 cups broccoli florets

1/4 cup beef broth (low sodium)

2 tbsp oyster sauce (sugar-free)

1 tbsp olive oil

1 garlic clove, minced

Salt and pepper to taste

M.C.: Stir-frying

Procedure:

Heat olive oil in a pan. Add garlic and beef, cook until browned.

Add broccoli, beef broth, and oyster sauce. Cover and simmer until broccoli is tender.

Serve over cauliflower rice for a complete meal.

N.V.: Calories: 220, Fat: 9g, Carbs: 5g, Protein: 29g.

Sweet Indulgences That Fit Your Diet

Recipe 1: Almond Flour Chocolate Chip Cookies

P.T.: 20 minutes

Ingr:

2 cups almond flour

1/2 cup erythritol

1 tsp baking powder

1/4 tsp salt

1/4 cup coconut oil, melted

1 large egg

1 tsp vanilla extract

1/2 cup sugar-free chocolate chips

M.C.: Baking

Procedure:

Preheat the oven to 350°F (175°C). Line a baking sheet with parchment paper.

In a bowl, mix almond flour, erythritol, baking powder, and salt.

Stir in melted coconut oil, egg, and vanilla extract until well combined.

Fold in chocolate chips.

Drop dough by spoonfuls onto the prepared baking sheet and flatten slightly.

Bake for 12-15 minutes or until edges are golden brown.

N.V.: Approximately per cookie: Calories: 160, Fat: 14g, Net Carbs: 2g, Protein: 4g.

Recipe 2: Berry Chia Pudding

P.T.: 15 minutes + chilling

Ingr:

1/4 cup chia seeds

1 cup unsweetened almond milk

1/2 tsp vanilla extract

1 tbsp erythritol (adjust to taste)

1/2 cup mixed berries (fresh or thawed from frozen)

M.C.: No-cook, Refrigeration

Procedure:

In a bowl, whisk together chia seeds, almond milk, vanilla extract, and erythritol.

Let the mixture sit for 5 minutes, then whisk again to prevent clumping.

Cover and refrigerate for at least 2 hours, or overnight, until it has thickened into a pudding consistency.

Serve topped with mixed berries.

N.V.: Approximately per serving: Calories: 120, Fat: 7g, Net Carbs: 5g, Protein: 4g.

Recipe 3: Greek Yogurt Cheesecake with Strawberry Compote

P.T.: 30 minutes + chilling

Ingr:

For the crust: 1 cup almond flour, 2 tbsp melted butter, 1 tbsp erythritol.

For the filling: 2 cups Greek yogurt, 1/4 cup erythritol, 1 tsp vanilla extract, 2 eggs.

For the compote: 1 cup strawberries, 1 tbsp erythritol, 1 tsp lemon juice.

M.C.: Baking

Procedure:

Preheat the oven to 325°F (163°C). Mix almond flour, butter, and erythritol for the crust and press into the bottom of a springform pan. Bake for 10 minutes.

Beat Greek yogurt, erythritol, vanilla, and eggs until smooth. Pour over the crust and bake for 25 minutes or until set.

For the compote, simmer strawberries, erythritol, and lemon juice over medium heat until thickened.

Cool the cheesecake and top with strawberry compote before serving.

N.V.: Approximately per serving: Calories: 180, Fat: 12g, Net Carbs: 6g, Protein: 10g.

Recipe 4: Lemon Ricotta Pancakes

P.T.: 20 minutes

Ingr:

1 cup almond flour

1/2 cup ricotta cheese

2 eggs

1/4 cup erythritol

Zest of 1 lemon

1/2 tsp baking powder

Butter or oil for frying

M.C.: Pan-frying

Procedure:

In a bowl, mix almond flour, ricotta, eggs, erythritol, lemon zest, and baking powder until smooth.

Heat a non-stick skillet over medium heat with a little butter or oil.

Spoon batter onto the skillet, cooking pancakes until bubbles form and edges are dry, then flip and cook until golden.

N.V.: Approximately per serving (3 pancakes): Calories: 250, Fat: 20g, Net Carbs: 4g, Protein: 12g.

Recipe 5: No-Bake Peanut Butter Energy Balls

P.T.: 15 minutes + chilling

Ingr:

1 cup unsweetened peanut butter

1/4 cup flaxseed meal

1/4 cup unsweetened shredded coconut

2 tbsp erythritol

1 tsp vanilla extract

Pinch of salt

M.C.: Mixing, Refrigeration

Procedure:

In a mixing bowl, combine all ingredients until well blended.

Roll the mixture into small balls and place on a baking sheet lined with parchment paper.

Chill in the refrigerator for at least 1 hour

before serving.

N.V.: Approximately per ball: Calories: 100, Fat: 8g, Net Carbs: 2g, Protein: 4g.

Recipe 6: Avocado Chocolate Mousse

P.T.: 10 minutes + chilling

Ingr:

2 ripe avocados

1/4 cup unsweetened cocoa powder

1/4 cup erythritol

1/2 cup unsweetened almond milk

1 tsp vanilla extract

M.C.: Blending

Procedure:

Blend all ingredients in a food processor until smooth.

Chill for at least 1 hour before serving.

N.V.: Approximately per serving: Calories: 200, Fat: 15g, Net Carbs: 5g, Protein: 3g.

Recipe 7: Cinnamon Almond Flour Apple Crisp

P.T.: 45 minutes

Ingr:

2 cups diced apples (skin on for fiber)

1 cup almond flour

1/4 cup erythritol

1/4 cup unsalted butter, cold and cubed

1 tsp cinnamon

Pinch of salt

M.C.: Baking

Procedure:

Preheat the oven to 350°F (175°C). Toss diced apples with cinnamon and a tablespoon of erythritol, place in a baking dish.

Mix almond flour, the remaining erythritol, salt, and butter until crumbly. Sprinkle over apples.

Bake for 30 minutes or until topping is golden and apples are tender.

N.V.: Approximately per serving: Calories: 220, Fat: 18g, Net Carbs: 8g, Protein: 4g.

Chapter 11: Building a Diabetic-Friendly Pantry

Essential Ingredients for Diabetic Baking

Creating a diabetic-friendly pantry is akin to building a solid foundation for a house. Without the right building blocks, no matter how grand the design, the structure won't stand the test of time—or in this case, support a healthy, balanced diet for those managing diabetes. At the core of diabetic baking lies the essence of smart, health-conscious choices that pivot around maintaining blood sugar levels while not compromising on taste and satisfaction.

The transformation from a regular pantry to one that's diabetic-friendly doesn't happen overnight, and it certainly doesn't mean you're left with bland, unappetizing options. It's about embracing a shift towards ingredients that are lower in carbohydrates, sugars, and have a minimal impact on blood glucose levels, yet are rich in flavor and versatility.

Flours are foundational in baking, but traditional white flour is high in carbohydrates and low in fiber, leading to spikes in blood sugar levels. Alternative flours, such as almond, coconut, and flaxseed meals, step in as the heroes. Almond flour, with its mild, nutty flavor, is not only low in carbs but also high in fiber and protein, making it an excellent choice for everything from bread to pastries. Coconut flour, another staple, is absorbent and lends a rich texture and sweetness to baked goods, allowing for reduced added sugar. Flaxseed meal, with its earthy tone, is packed with omega-3 fatty acids, fiber, and lignans, making it beneficial for heart health as well as blood sugar management.

Sweeteners play a pivotal role in the enjoyment of desserts, but for those managing diabetes, traditional sugars are a path best avoided. Nature offers us a bounty of alternatives that can sweeten without the accompanying glucose spike. Stevia, a plant-based sweetener, provides a sugar-like sweetness without the calories or carbohydrates. Erythritol, a sugar alcohol, is another favorite, having 70% of the sweetness of sugar but virtually no calories or impact on blood sugar levels. Monk fruit sweetener, derived from the luo han guo fruit, is yet another option, offering sweetness without bitterness, and it's suitable for both cooking and baking.

Beyond flours and sweeteners, a diabetic-friendly pantry is rounded out with other essentials that enhance flavor and nutritional value. Unsweetened cocoa powder and dark chocolate, rich in antioxidants, provide that chocolatey indulgence without the sugar rush. Nuts and seeds add crunch and nutrition, offering healthy fats, fiber, and protein. Spices and extracts, such as cinnamon, vanilla, and almond extract, bring depth and complexity to desserts without adding sugar or calories.

Incorporating these ingredients into your baking repertoire opens a world of possibilities. Imagine a chocolate cake, moist and rich, yet made with almond flour and sweetened with erythritol, or a batch of cookies, crunchy and satisfying, yet devoid of traditional sugar, crafted with flaxseed meal and sweetened with stevia. These aren't just substitutions; they're transformations that allow for indulgence without compromise.

Understanding the characteristics and best uses of these ingredients is crucial. Almond flour, for instance, requires more egg or binding agent to hold together, given its lack of gluten. Coconut flour's absorbency means you'll need to adjust liquid ingredients in recipes to avoid dryness. Learning these nuances is part of the journey, transforming baking from a routine to an exploration of flavors and textures.

Transitioning to a diabetic-friendly pantry is not just about swapping ingredients; it's about reimagining what dessert means. It's a commitment to health without giving up the joy of baking and indulgence. Each ingredient in the pantry becomes a tool for creativity, a way to explore new tastes, and a step towards managing diabetes with delight rather than deprivation. This approach to baking empowers individuals to enjoy dessert, knowing they're nourishing their body with every bite.

In crafting a diabetic-friendly pantry, the goal is not to restrict but to expand the horizon of possibilities. It's about creating a space where every ingredient serves a purpose, supporting health and wellness without sacrificing flavor. It's a testament to the fact that with the right ingredients, diabetic baking can be just as satisfying, if not more so, than traditional methods. This foundational shift in the pantry is not just a change in ingredients; it's a change in perspective, where every meal can be a step towards better health.

Reading Labels: What to Look For and What to Avoid

Navigating the world of food labels can be a complex journey, especially for those managing diabetes. Understanding what to look for and what to avoid is crucial in maintaining a balanced and healthy diet. When we talk about reading labels, it's not just about the numbers; it's about understanding the ingredients and their impact on blood sugar levels.

Firstly, let's dive into the world of carbohydrates. They're not all created equal. The type, quality, and quantity of carbs in food can affect blood sugar levels differently. Whole grains, for instance, are absorbed more slowly, preventing spikes in blood sugar. When reading labels, look for whole grain ingredients at the top of the list, such as whole wheat flour or oats. These ingredients provide essential fiber, which aids in blood sugar regulation.

Sugar alcohols like xylitol, erythritol, and sorbitol are often found in "sugar-free" products. While they have less impact on blood sugar than regular sugar, they can cause digestive issues if consumed in large amounts. It's important to balance the benefits of lower blood sugar impact with potential digestive discomfort.

Understanding fats is also crucial. Not all fats are the enemy. Healthy fats from avocados, nuts, and seeds can be beneficial, but it's important to avoid trans fats and limit saturated fats. These can be found in processed foods and baked goods. Look for terms like "partially hydrogenated oils" on labels, a key indicator of trans fats, and steer clear.

Sodium is another ingredient to watch. High sodium intake can increase blood pressure, which is already a concern for those with diabetes. The American Diabetes Association recommends limiting sodium intake to 2,300 mg a day, or even less for better heart health. When reading labels, compare products and choose those with lower sodium content.

Lastly, artificial sweeteners, while not affecting blood sugar levels directly, can still have an impact on your health and cravings. Products labeled as "diet" or "sugar-free" might seem appealing, but it's essential to consider their overall nutritional value and potential effects on your eating habits.

In conclusion, managing diabetes involves more than just counting carbs or calories. It requires a holistic approach to nutrition, understanding the ingredients in your food, and how they affect your body. Reading labels is a skill that can help you make informed choices, contributing to a healthier lifestyle and better diabetes management.

Planning and Preparing Diabetic-Friendly Desserts Ahead of Time

Planning and preparing diabetic-friendly desserts ahead of time is an art and science that requires foresight, creativity, and a good understanding of how different ingredients interact to affect blood sugar levels. The key is to embrace the process as a joyful exploration rather than a restriction, allowing you to savor your favorite treats without compromising your health.

Imagine having a pantry stocked with almond and coconut flour, instead of traditional white flour, to provide a lower glycemic index base for your recipes. These flours not only add a rich, nutty flavor to your desserts but also increase the fiber content, which is beneficial for blood sugar control.

Sweeteners play a critical role in diabetic-friendly desserts. Utilizing natural sweeteners like stevia, erythritol, or monk fruit extract can offer the sweetness we crave, without the blood sugar spike associated with traditional sugar. Each of these has its unique flavor profile and baking properties, offering a range of options to suit different tastes and recipes.

Incorporating high-fiber fruits and vegetables, such as berries, apples with their skin, and pumpkin, can add natural sweetness and moisture to desserts, along with a nutritional boost. These ingredients not only enhance the flavor but also contribute to the overall fiber content, helping to slow down the absorption of sugars.

Fats are another essential component to consider. Healthy fats, like those from avocados, nuts, and seeds, can be used to add moisture and richness to desserts. They also help to slow the absorption of carbohydrates, making them a crucial element in diabetic-friendly baking.

Spices and flavorings, such as cinnamon, vanilla, and cocoa powder, not only add depth and complexity to your desserts but can also provide health benefits. Cinnamon, for example, is known for its ability to help control blood sugar levels. By planning your desserts ahead of time, you can ensure that you have all the necessary ingredients on hand to create delicious, healthy treats whenever the mood strikes.

This approach allows you to experiment with different recipes and ingredient combinations, discovering new favorites that satisfy your sweet tooth without compromising your dietary goals. Creating diabetic-friendly desserts is more than just a culinary endeavor; it's a way to enjoy life's sweet moments while managing diabetes effectively. It's about making thoughtful choices that align with your health goals, without feeling deprived of the joys of baking and indulging in sweet treats. With the right ingredients and a bit of planning, you can create a range of desserts that are not only safe for those managing diabetes but also delicious and satisfying for everyone to enjoy.

Conclusion

Tips for Enjoying Desserts While Managing Diabetes

Embracing the sweet side of life while managing diabetes requires a blend of knowledge, creativity, and moderation. Enjoying desserts as part of a diabetes-friendly lifestyle isn't about strict denial or unattainable standards; it's about making informed choices that allow you to indulge in a way that supports your health and well-being.

Firstly, the key to incorporating desserts into a diabetic diet is to understand the impact of ingredients on blood sugar levels and to make adjustments accordingly. This involves selecting natural sweeteners with a lower glycemic index, such as stevia or monk fruit extract, which can sweeten a dessert without causing a significant spike in blood sugar. Equally important is the choice of whole, nutrient-dense ingredients like almond flour or coconut flour instead of traditional refined flours, which not only add fiber but also help slow the absorption of sugar into the bloodstream.

Portion control is another crucial aspect of enjoying desserts while managing diabetes. It allows for the pleasure of sweet treats without overindulging, which is essential for maintaining balanced blood sugar levels. A practical approach is to savor smaller portions of desserts, focusing on the enjoyment of each bite and the flavors, rather than the quantity of the dessert itself.

Incorporating a balance of nutrients in dessert recipes can also make them more diabetes-friendly. For example, adding nuts or seeds can introduce healthy fats and protein, which help to moderate blood sugar levels and provide a sustained sense of fullness. This balanced approach to dessert-making ensures that treats can be enjoyed without compromising dietary goals.

Furthermore, timing can play a significant role in how desserts impact blood sugar levels. Enjoying a small dessert after a meal that includes fiber, protein, and healthy fats can help minimize blood sugar spikes, as these nutrients slow down the digestion and absorption of sugars.

Finally, staying active and monitoring blood sugar levels before and after consuming desserts can help you understand how your body responds to different ingredients and portion sizes. This awareness allows for more personalized and informed decisions about how to include desserts in a diabetes-friendly diet.

Enjoying desserts while managing diabetes is an art that emphasizes mindfulness, moderation, and the joy of eating. By focusing on quality ingredients, portion control, and the overall balance of nutrients, it's possible to indulge in sweet treats that satisfy cravings without compromising health. This approach not only supports physical well-being but also enhances the quality of life, proving that a diagnosis of diabetes can still include the sweetness of life's many pleasures.

How to Adapt Your Favorite Recipes to Be More Diabetic-Friendly

Adapting your favorite recipes to be more diabetic-friendly is a journey of creativity and experimentation, allowing you to savor the tastes you love while managing your blood sugar levels. The essence of this transformation lies in the careful selection and substitution of ingredients, mindful of their impact on health without compromising on flavor.

At the heart of this adaptation process is the innovative use of sweeteners. Traditional sugar can be replaced with alternatives like stevia, erythritol, or monk fruit extract, which offer the sweetness without the same blood sugar spike. Each sweetener has its unique properties and ratios for substitution, so experimenting to find the perfect balance for your palate is key.

Flour also plays a pivotal role in baking. Swapping out white flour for almond, coconut, or oat flour not only reduces the carbohydrate content but also enhances the nutritional profile of your desserts. These flours bring a new dimension of flavor and texture, making your treats both delicious and nutritious.

Incorporating fiber-rich ingredients is another strategy to make recipes more diabetic-friendly. Fiber slows down the absorption of sugar into the bloodstream, providing stability to blood sugar levels. Ingredients like chia seeds, flaxseeds, or pureed fruits and vegetables can add moisture and fiber to recipes, improving both the healthfulness and taste of your desserts.

Fat is an essential component for adding richness and satiety to desserts. Opting for healthy fats such as avocado oil, olive oil, or nut butters can improve the fatty acid profile of your desserts, making them more conducive to a heart-healthy diabetic diet.

Lastly, the art of recipe adaptation extends beyond just the ingredients. Portion control, serving size, and the timing of dessert consumption play crucial roles in how desserts fit into a diabetic-friendly lifestyle. Smaller portions allow for indulgence without excess, and enjoying sweets as part of a balanced meal can help mitigate spikes in blood sugar.

By approaching recipe adaptation with an open mind and a willingness to experiment, you can transform your favorite treats into versions that align with your dietary needs. This process not only preserves the joy of baking and dessert-making but also empowers you to maintain a balanced and healthful diet.

Encouragement for a Balanced and Sweet Life

Embracing a balanced and sweet life, especially when managing diabetes, is a journey that combines mindfulness, joy, and a commitment to health. It's about finding harmony between the foods you love and the choices that nurture your well-being. This balance isn't about strict limitations or denying yourself the pleasures of delicious desserts. Instead, it's about embracing a holistic approach to health that includes enjoying treats in moderation, being creative with ingredients, and making informed choices that support your diabetes management.

Living a balanced life means recognizing that food is not just fuel but also a source of joy and celebration. It's important to allow yourself the freedom to enjoy desserts while also understanding how they fit into your overall dietary pattern. This might mean choosing desserts with lower sugar content, using alternative sweeteners, or simply being mindful of portion sizes.

Moreover, maintaining a sweet life with diabetes emphasizes the importance of regular physical activity, stress management, and connecting with a supportive community. These elements complement your dietary choices, helping to manage blood sugar levels and enhance your overall quality of life.

Encouragement in this journey comes from knowing you're not alone. Many have navigated this path before, finding ways to enjoy life's sweetness without compromising their health. Sharing recipes, tips, and experiences with others can provide motivation and inspiration, making the journey more enjoyable and sustainable.

Ultimately, living a balanced and sweet life with diabetes is about making choices that reflect your values, preferences, and health goals. It's about enjoying the richness of life, with all its flavors, in a way that feels good and supports your health. This approach not only enriches your life but also empowers you to manage diabetes with confidence and positivity.

BONUS: Sweet Seasons Diabetic - Friendly Desserts Through the Year

Made in the USA
Las Vegas, NV
28 August 2024

94556767R00063